Hold On, You Lost Me!
Use Learning Styles to Create
Training That Sticks

Bernice McCarthy and
Jeanine O'Neill-Blackwell

ASTD PRESS

Alexandria, VA

ASTD Press is an internationally renowned source of insightful and practical information on workplace learning and performance topics, including training basics, evaluation and return-on-investment (ROI), instructional systems development (ISD), e-learning, leadership, and career development.

Ordering information: Books published by ASTD Press can be purchased by visiting our website at store.astd.org or by calling 800.628.2783 or 703.683.8100.

Library of Congress Control Number: 2007921488

ISBN-10: 1-56286-497-1
ISBN-13: 978-1-56286- 497-2

ASTD Press Editorial Staff
Director: Cat Russo
Manager, Acquisitions & Author Development: Mark Morrow
Editorial Manager: Jacqueline Edlund-Braun
Editorial Assistant: Kelly Norris
Retail Trade Specialist: Nancy Silva

Copyeditor: April Michelle Davis
Indexer: Robert Elwood
Proofreader: Ann Lee Bruen
Interior Design and Production: Stephen McDougal
Cover Design: Ana Ilieva and Imaginal Marketing
Cover Illustration: René Mansi
Printed by Victor Graphics, Inc., Baltimore, Maryland, www.victorgraphics.com.

Beth Lienhart

Dedication

"The master in the art of living makes little distinction between his work and his play, his labor and his leisure, his mind and his body, his information and his recreation, his love and his religion. He hardly knows which is which. He simply pursues his vision of excellence at whatever he does, leaving others to decide whether he is working or playing. To him he's always doing both."

—James A. Michener

To the About Learning Team who inspire me every day.

—Bernice McCarthy

To Terry, Madison, Mackensie, and Riley…. You inspire me to live, work, play, and love with all my being.

—Jeanine O'Neill-Blackwell

Contents

Preface

The Learning Process

Chances are you picked up this book because you are someone who designs training, delivers training, or leads a team of trainers. Whether you design, train, or lead, the process the learner is engaged in is the same: learning. The better you understand your own way of learning, how others learn, and what happens when learning really takes place, the better trainer, presenter, and leader you will be.

The framework we will share in this book is based on one of the most widely used instructional models in the K–12 education market. More than 600,000 educators, trainers, and learners have experienced the learning style assessment that you will experience in this book. This model is a powerful and proven model for understanding how learning happens and how to reach all learners.

What Is Learning?

Learning is a process that involves the perceiving and processing of information. It is the process of taking in information, reflecting on that information, making judgments based on the information, and acting on those judgments. By this definition, when we scan an email, prepare a report, write a letter, deliver a presentation, or interview someone, we are learning.

Each of us has a preferred way of perceiving and processing experiences—of interacting with our world. We call this a learning style. A learning style is a description of consistent preferences each of us has for the way we like to receive, process, and package information.

How do we develop these preferences? Our preferred way of learning is based on what has worked successfully for us in the past. This dominant way of perceiving and processing information provides us with some real advantages:

- **Our dominant approach saves us time and effort.** The more we travel a familiar path, the easier it is for us to travel it. We don't have to spend much time figuring out how to approach a situation or decision if we default to our dominant approach. This is a lot like driving to work. Every day most of us drive the same route to work. We could always find a more creative way of getting there— if we wanted to. It just would take longer and require more mental energy.
- **We get better at our way of knowing.** Our biceps respond to repeated activity and so do our brains. By consistently approaching new situations from our dominant perspective, we become more skilled in our way of knowing.
- **Our learning styles define our approach to learning.** Our learning styles ease us into one kind of thinking and doing and are obstacles to other kinds. We tend to hang around longer in the parts of the learning process where the learning is easy, and often avoid the parts of the learning process that call for stretching. Those stretching places force us to exert energy and intentionally focus. One learning style excels in discussion and sharing, another in lecture and reading, another in hands-on problem solving, and a fourth in real-world performance learning. Very few of us excel in all four without real attention to stretching, and our training styles are closely linked to our learning style preferences. Our strength areas are our source of power, as leaders and trainers. By identifying opportunity areas that we can stretch to, we will maximize our abilities to create transformational learning, whether it is within a team or the four walls of a classroom.
- **Our learning styles affect our approaches to training.** Every learner has a favored style. Every style seeks a different type of learning experience. Every style will evaluate the same experience differently. Most trainers refine their training skills by observing and emulating trainers whom they perceive as highly effective. The interesting twist to this is that our learning styles determine what we define as effective learning. When trainers emulate other trainers they find particularly engaging, they are often reinforcing their natural areas of strength. Once we recognize our learning/training styles, we will be able to identify and integrate new skills and techniques that will improve our abilities to engage all learners, not just those that enjoy our natural styles.
- **Once we understand our styles and others' styles, our abilities to understand and honor others are greatly enhanced.** Instead of wishing your colleagues

(and sometimes family members) would become more like us, we will come to honor and seek out those who bring different insights and ways of knowing to the process. We will begin to identify how other styles complement our thinking processes. We may even find that the learners we find most challenging hold the greatest opportunity to stretch us.

- **Learning styles directly influence career choices.** Those who are delighted in training and would do it even if they weren't paid are working in something that is highly compatible with their preferred styles. Likewise, a given profession tends to attract the same learning style. The way professions are taught attracts those who have a way of learning that matches the teaching methodology. The core processing skills required in certain fields also draw learners with a particular preference for that processing style.

If you are a trainer who works in a specific industry or particular functional area, the tendency for certain styles to cluster in specific roles may have a great effect on the type of learners who are dominating your classes. You may find that learners with different learning styles will experience the same workshop and rate it differently. Once you recognize the types of learners in your classes, you can better adapt content and delivery to reach all of them. This book will help you identify techniques and skills you can use to reach every learner every time.

What This Book Will Do For You

This book will

- **Show you how you learn and how others learn.** We will help you understand and recognize learning styles—what they are, their origins, why they are important, and why every trainer should know how to capitalize on them. In chapter 1, you will have an opportunity to assess your own style using the Learning Type Measure descriptions. Your style greatly influences how you design, deliver, and evaluate training. It also affects the type of learners that are most engaged, and most disengaged, by your natural training style.

- **Help you identify where you can improve your training skills.** Your learning style affects how you train. As trainers, we tend to design and deliver training that appeals to our own learning style preferences. In this book, you will identify your training style and your natural training strengths, develop a strategy for enhancing your training skill in all parts of the learning and training process, and explore practical tips and techniques that you can apply to help you reach all types of learners, regardless of your natural style.

- **Help you consistently design effective training.** The 4MAT Model is an eight-step process for designing effective training. When you address each of the eight steps in the design and delivery process, you will engage every learner. This book will explain how to effectively address each of the eight steps. You will also find examples of effective training designs that use the 4MAT Model.

- **Enhance your delivery skills.**

As this book will show, you will need to focus on all the parts of the Learning Cycle. Icons have been placed in areas that relate to a specific part of the Learning Cycle, which will help you focus on your weaker areas.

This icon will point out specifics about the preferences of the Type One learners and what happens in the first part of the Learning Cycle, Engage.

This icon will point out specifics about the preferences of the Type Two learners and what happens in the second part of the Learning Cycle, Share.

This icon will point out specifics about the preferences of the Type Three learners and what happens in the third part of the Learning Cycle, Practice.

This icon will point out specifics about the preferences of the Type Four learners and what happens in the fourth part of the Learning Cycle, Perform.

In addition, at the end of each chapter, there is an exercise to help you "stretch" to become a better, more successful trainer. These activities will be marked with the following icon.

The focus, activities, and techniques a trainer uses in the beginning, middle, and end of a training session shift significantly in well-delivered training. The 4MAT Model explains what an effective trainer is doing in each part of the learning process. In this book, you will identify key focus areas and techniques in each part of the learning process.

We will begin by explaining how learning happens. There is a natural flow to learning—the Learning Cycle. Your learning style refers to the part of the Learning Cycle that you enjoy the most. You will have an opportunity to assess your learning style. Once you understand learning styles, we will explore how your learning style affects your training style. You will also learn how to apply this knowledge to designing and delivering effective training that sticks.

Chapter 1

Learning Styles and the 4MAT Model

⸻⸻⸻⸻⸻⸻⸻⸻⸻⸻⸻⸻⸻⸻▶

We all perceive and then process our experiences, along with the information gained from the experiences. The differences in the way we approach these two activities define our learning styles. This chapter will explore how this basic fact of all human learning can have a profound influence on the way we deliver training.

Perceiving: The First Activity

Some of us perceive strongly by sensing and feeling. Those of us who do, enjoy being in the experience, enjoy immersing ourselves in the process, and seek to personally connect to the experience. Others sense and feel also, but move quickly to thinking and judging. There is a big difference in these two ways of taking in information.

Imagine you have never experienced or even heard about a type of fruit called an "orange." You are eager to learn about oranges. If you were a strong senser/feeler, you would smell it, scratch it, and tear it open. You would notice the juice running down your arms and taste it. You would peel the sections apart and plop one in your mouth. You would notice the sweet and slightly tart taste. If you were a senser/feeler, you would enjoy this way of learning about oranges and spend a lot of time experiencing the orange.

You might also look up the word "orange" in the dictionary or get on the Internet and research "oranges." You would find that an orange is

1. (a) any of several southeast Asian evergreen trees of the genus Citrus, having fragrant white flowers and round fruit with a yellowish or reddish rind and a

sectioned pulpy interior; or (b) the fruit of any of these trees, having a sweet-ish acidic juice

2. any of several similar plants, such as the mock orange
3. color. The hue of the portion of the visible spectrum lying between red and yellow with wavelengths of approximately 590–630 nanometers.

This type of learning is thinking/judging. If you preferred thinking and judging, you might skip the sensing/feeling and move right into researching oranges and finding out what the experts can tell you about them.

How do you prefer to perceive or take in information? Would you rather immerse yourself in an experience? Or would you rather research, read, or learn from the experts? Your preference for feeling or thinking greatly influences what type of learning grabs your interest.

Processing: The Second Activity

After we perceive, we process our experience. Some of us spend more time watching and reflecting before acting on our judgments. Others spend little time watching and reflecting and, instead, move right into action. Clearly, there are positives and negatives in both ways of processing. Watching takes longer but may produce a better outcome. Doing is more at risk for error but gets the job done quickly. If you like to reflect and ponder, you are a Watcher. If you prefer to jump in and get your hands in it, you are a Doer.

As a trainer, you must recognize the difference in these two types of learners. The learners in your workshops who are Watchers are going to hang back. They are going to wait and see. They want total clarity on the information before you ask them to do something with it. They want to know that they know. They might even seem a little bored if you measure engagement by questions asked and how interactive they are in dialogue.

The Doers are bored, that is, if all you do is talk about the content. They prefer to do it, rather than talk about it. They want to process through activity. As you are presenting, they are envisioning how they might use the information. When you assign an activity, they are the first to jump in. Many times, they don't even wait for all of the directions. They are active learners who seek application.

> "All of our knowledge has its origins in our perceptions."
>
> —Leonardo da Vinci

How do you process information? Would you rather figure it out first, then move into action? Or do you prefer to jump in and learn as you go?

> "Perception is real, even when it is not reality."
> —Edward de Bono

The questions of whether you prefer to feel or think when you perceive and whether you prefer to watch or do when you process are significant questions. The answers to these questions are important to both your success as a trainer and the success of your learners.

Your Learning Style

When you combine the preference for feeling or thinking with the preference for watching or doing, you find four distinct preference combinations. These four combinations are the basis of the 4MAT Model and are the Learning Type Measure descriptions.

Compare the descriptions of your own style results with table 1-1 on the next page. These descriptions of the four major learning styles are based on a compilation of the research of Kolb, Piaget, Dewey, Jung, Lawrence, Myers-Briggs, and McCarthy. Which one do you favor? Read the descriptions of the learning styles in table 1-1, and underline any word, phrase, or sentence that you can say, "This is really me."

Your Style

Reflect for a moment on your style, and answer the questions below. You may find it helpful to share your reflections with someone.

- Which of the four is most like you?
- Is there a second one that is close to your preference?
- Which one is definitely not you?
- Think about the people in your life. What are their learning styles?
- What type of people would most enjoy the type of learning experiences you design or deliver?
- Think about the people you most enjoy working with. What do you think their learning styles are?
- What type of people do you enjoy having in your training?
- Do these answers tell you anything about yourself?

Some Common Questions

There are two styles that both seem to equally describe me. Is that normal?

Table 1-1. Learning style characteristics.

Type Four: Dynamic Learners

- Seek hidden possibilities.
- Need to know what can be done with things.
- Learn by trial and error, self-discovery.
- Enrich reality.
- Perceive information concretely, and process it actively.
- Adapt to change and relish it, like variety, and excel in situations calling for flexibility; tend to take risks; at ease with people but sometimes seen as pushy; often reach accurate conclusions in the absence of logical justification.
- Function by acting and testing experience.
- Strength: Action, carrying out plans
- Goals: To make things happen, to bring action to concept
- Favorite question: "If"

Type One: Imaginative Learners

- Seek meaning.
- Need to be involved personally.
- Learn by listening and sharing ideas.
- Absorb reality.
- Perceive information concretely, and process it reflectively.
- Are interested in people and culture. They are divergent thinkers who believe in their own experiences, excel in viewing concrete situations from many perspectives, and model themselves on those they respect.
- Function through social interaction.
- Are idea people.
- Strength: Innovating and imagination
- Goals: Self-involvement in important issues, bringing unity to diversity
- Favorite question: "Why"

Type Three: Common Sense Learners

- Seek usability.
- Need to know how things work.
- Learn by testing theories in ways that seem sensible.
- Edit reality.
- Receive information abstractly, and process it actively.
- Use factual data to build designed concepts. They need hands-on experiences, enjoy solving problems, resent being given answers, restrict judgment to concrete things, and have limited tolerance for fuzzy ideas. They need to know how things they are asked to do will help in real life.
- Function through inferences drawn from sensory experience.
- Strength: Practical application of ideas
- Goals: To bring their views of the presentation into line
- Favorite question: "How"

Type Two: Analytic Learners

- Seek facts.
- Need to know what the experts think.
- Learn by thinking through ideas.
- Form reality.
- Perceive information abstractly, and process it reflectively.
- Are less interested in people, ideas, and concepts; they critique information and are data collectors. Thorough and industrious, they will re-examine facts if situations perplex them.
- Benefit the most from schools.
- Function by adapting to experts.
- Strength: Creating concepts and models
- Goals: Self-satisfaction and intellectual recognition
- Favorite question: "What"

Reprinted with permission from Aboutlearning.com. The 4MAT Learning Type Measure was normed with the MBTI and the Kolb LSI. To complete a 4MAT Learning Type Measure, go to www.4MAT4Business.com

---

Learning Styles in the Workplace

Learning is the process of taking in information and processing it. Take a look at how learning styles can show up in work situations:

Example 1

You are an innovative risk-taker, and you trust your intuitive, decision-making track record. Mark is your point person in accounting. You are working on a project team together. Mark is a careful, reflective thinker who trusts the data, seldom venturing into his intuitive side, actually wary of it. The meeting you are having badly needs a fast decision. You are convinced of the action the company needs to take. Mark is stalling any action with his need for foolproof data. What do you do?

Example 2

You are a fast-thinking, bottom-line-oriented president of a small company. Your second-in-command, Lee Ann, is a people person who believes strongly that everyone should be in agreement before undertaking any new program. You hired Lee Ann because of her intelligence and genuineness. You felt, at some intuitive level, that you needed her patient facilitation skills to sustain the ongoing success of your company. This has worked well. Now, however, the competitive landscape is changing, and your company needs to make changes quickly. Lee Ann's insistence on unanimous decision making has become a real problem. What do you do?

Example 3

You are responsible for the sales team of a medium-sized pharmaceutical company. Jim, the team leader of the accounting department, has just issued a new set of procedures for expense reimbursement. After receiving the memo, your sales team is balking at the ludicrousness of getting approval for any expense over $50. After fielding several complaints from sales team members who suggest the accountants come "out in the field and see how the money really gets made," you must decide how to approach Jim for a resolution. What do you do?

You may have found that there are two styles that seem to describe your learning approach. Below are some common combinations of styles:

- Type One-Four learners have high people skills in nurturing and influencing.
- Type Two-Three learners combine theory and application extremely well.
- Type Three-Four learners, entrepreneur types, generate ideas and ask, "Will this really work?"

If you are a strong combination of two styles, notice what elements of each style most describe you. You may discover that one of these two styles is dominant in different processes.

Reflect for a moment on your style, and think about significant people in your life. What style might they be?

Is One Learning Style More Effective in a Training Role Than Another?

The key to being an effective trainer is the ability to satisfy the needs of every learning type. Every trainer, regardless of learning style, has the opportunity to consciously incorporate tools and techniques that successfully engage all learning styles.

> "Everything that irritates us about others can lead us to an understanding about ourselves."
>
> —Carl Jung

The 4MAT Model Learning Cycle is a four-part model that explains how learning happens. This book explains what happens in all four parts of the learning process: engage, share, practice, and perform. You will also learn how each style has a preference for one part of the learning process over the others. For now, you should understand how your learning style affects your definition of effective learning and how this might differ from how other styles define effective learning.

To illustrate the difference in learner preferences, imagine you are observing a group of learners in a training workshop. By simply observing learner behavior, you can recognize how learning styles affect learner engagement. Take a look at the descriptions of the four learners below. Do any of these descriptions sound like learners you have experienced in your training classes?

 1. Grace is an imaginative, Type One learner. She prefers to be connected with others. She loves interacting in small groups, discussing meaningful issues. She enjoys stories and meaningful dialogue. She enjoys authentic, personal trainers who she perceives to have high integrity. She sometimes struggles with putting what she is learning into action, preferring to reflect before moving into activity.

 2. Sam is an analytic, Type Two learner. He prefers facts and sequential thinking. He loves organized lecture, but sometimes struggles with visionary thinking or random ideas being interjected into the discussion. He prefers to stay on track with the agenda and follow along in the workbook. He enjoys credible, well-organized trainers who deliver well-researched content.

 3. Anita is a hands-on, Type Three learner. She loves problem solving, but sometimes struggles with touchy-feely content. If she never had to participate in another icebreaker activity again, that would be fine with her. She often prefers to do activities herself, to save time and reduce frustration. She enjoys trainers who have real-world experience with a focus on practical application.

4. John is a dynamic, Type Four learner. He loves spontaneity and the freedom to explore random ideas, but sometimes struggles with staying on task. He likes to interject his own insights into the dialogue. He enjoys trainers who create dynamic learning environments and encourage creative thinking.

Each of these learners will find different types of activities engaging. One learner type will enjoy skits and role plays, and another will prefer to sit quietly and read. Recognizing and addressing these differences is key to effective training design and delivery.

IS YOUR LEARNING STYLE A STRENGTH OR WEAKNESS?

You might be asking yourself, "Is it good to be a Type Four trainer or a Type Two trainer?" Your learning style is a natural strength when presenting to other learners

---

Stretching Exercises

- Seek out colleagues with different learning styles. Use each other's strengths to improve your ability to design and deliver effective training.

- Share training designs; videotape your training sessions; ask others to contribute to refining your training materials. Look for ways to receive feedback from people with different learning perspectives.

- Pay special attention to posttraining reaction surveys. Learner feedback can often help to identify patterns of training style. Notice if there is a particular part of the Learning Cycle that needs more focus in your training design and delivery.

- When you are creating or involved in project teams, look at the learning style mix of the team. Well-balanced teams with good representation of each learning style produce the best results. If the primary team you work with leans toward one or two styles, be conscious of what you tend to focus on and value. Notice what you tend to skip or avoid.

- Invite guest colleagues with different learning styles into your meetings for input and refinement of the processes you are designing and implementing.

- In the training environment, consciously move people around into different groups. This forces participants to interact with different styles. It also gives the facilitator an opportunity to report observations about the effect the learning style has on the activities in the workshop.

- Be aware that we often seek out people who share our perspective for feedback because they often give us validation. Instead, when looking for someone to bounce ideas off of, seek out people who have different learning styles. By seeking out different perspectives, you will expand your own perspective.

> "What we see depends mainly on what we look for."
> —Sir John Lubbock

who have similar preferences. You will naturally design activities that you, and others with similar styles, will find appealing. Your style can quickly become a weakness when presenting to others with different learning styles. Your definition of an effective learning experience can differ greatly from others with different learning styles. The key to overcoming this weakness is to adopt techniques that stretch you toward your less dominant styles.

The tension that exists between the different ways of learning is a healthy means to balance thinking—both your own thinking process and an organization's thinking process. Once learners recognize how to stretch their thinking, they can apply the skills to any experience that involves taking in information and processing it. Learning styles apply to any process that involves sharing and receiving information, including coaching, team building, conflict resolution, and customer relations. Learning style is not a limiting label. On the contrary, it is a means to identify concrete ways to expand potential. And, at the heart of training is helping individuals and organizations reach their potential. Stretching, for learners, is an important part of growth.

Why is stretching so important? Why not just group learners by type? Or have Type Three trainers teach Type Three learners? Effective learning transfer requires that we engage in processes that are not always comfortable. By stretching into these uncomfortable places, as learners and as trainers, we grow. You need only to look opposite of your style on the cycle to identify the type of learning you find most painful.

Type One learners are generally not comfortable in the part of the learning process that Type Three learners enjoy most. Type Three learners are generally not comfortable in the part of the learning process that Type One learners enjoy most. The same is true for Type Two and Four learners.

There is productive tension between these opposite ways of knowing and learning. You can readily see how one style's way of thinking and learning balances the other, as shown in figure 1-1. Becoming aware of our strengths and complementing them by stretching to opposite ways of knowing improves our thinking and, ultimately, our training skills.

Figure 1-1. Opposite styles.

Four Questions All Learners Ask

Each style has a core question that drives a person's approach to learning. These four questions, as shown in table 1-2, drive the learning process. Answering these questions, as a learner and as a trainer, generates better, thought-out solutions and more complete learning.

Type Three learners learn by answering the question, "How." They like to jump in and figure things out as they go. The counterbalance to the Type Three learners' need for action is the need to take time for reflection. Type One learners' favorite question, "Why," encourages the reflection that balances the Type Three learners' need for action. When you balance the "Why" and the "How," the result is both effective and efficient.

The same is true of the opposite styles of Type Two and Four learners. The "If" questions that Type Four learners ask are perfectly balanced by the "What" questions Type Two learners ask. The Type Two thought process grounds the Type Four thought

Table 1-2. Learner questions.

Learner Type	Favorite Questions
One	Why?
Two	What?
Three	How?
Four	If?

Jeanine on Stretching

 Earlier in my career, one of my responsibilities involved facilitating a corporate university leadership program for customers, vendors, and employees. The program was highly regarded in our industry, and people traveled from around the country to attend. It was a 16-day program, so the commitment level of the participants was very high. The participants described the program, as "inspiring" and "life-changing." The results were measured by the development of great relationships and the creation of shared vision for our industry and our collective businesses.

During the course of one of these programs, one of the participants, David, shared his experience with me. "I think you are great. You're good in the front of the room and all this stuff is very interesting, but I am so frustrated that I am not learning anything. There are lots of great ideas, but I feel like we are all over the place and have no plan. I want to know what to do with this when I get back (to my business). I need this broken down in a way that I can apply it."

David knew there was more I could bring to the process, and he was right. I was measuring my effectiveness through my definition of "effective"—innovation, meaning, and connection. David expanded that definition to include structure and results orientation. This conversation inspired me to stretch to my uncomfortable place.

---

process in reality. The Type Four thought process expands the Type Two learners' concepts of what is possible.

Tension between the styles is a big idea. When learners recognize their strengths and are encouraged to focus on the parts of the learning cycle that they avoid, the outcome of the learning is greater. In the next chapter, you will learn why all parts of the Learning Cycle need to be addressed to create an effective training.

Your Learning Workshop: Stretching Your Learning Style

Below are some easy ways to build your skills in your weaker areas of the Learning Cycle. Look at your learning style, and see where you can stretch.

Type One Learners

- Focus on procedures and specific outcomes.
- Act more quickly.
- Share your thoughts, as well as your feelings.
- Spend time on how to do it.
- Make ideas workable.
- Deal with conflict.
- Spend time planning.
- Try new things.
- Look at the bottom line.
- Challenge lack of closure.

Type Two Learners

- Try some action before you have a perfect plan.
- Take some risks.
- Be open to change.
- Go with your instincts.
- Share your questions with others.
- Be outgoing.
- Open your mind to other possibilities.
- Dare to experience the unknown.
- Inspire others.
- Challenge complacency.

Type Three Learners

- Chat with people about what is going on.
- Honor the process.
- Share your feelings with others.

- Look for the values in ideas.
- Consider that other ideas may be possible before coming to closure.
- Imagine.
- Allow others to find their own meaning.
- Weigh alternative possibilities.
- Challenge action for its own sake.

Type Four Learners

- Focus on structure.
- Reflect before acting.
- Show care for systems and procedures.
- Spend time on what to do.
- Think strategically.
- Appreciate that others have a low tolerance for change.
- Develop a model to structure your insights.
- Communicate your thinking process.
- Choose what risks to take.
- Challenge disorganization.

Chapter 2

The Learning Cycle

To better understand how your learning style affects your training effectiveness, let's begin by exploring what happens in the learning process.

The Learning Process

Learning is more complete if we

- experience, feel, and connect to our lives (Engage)
- reflect deeply and learn what the experts have to share (Share)
- take action based on our new understandings (Practice)
- refine the learning to make it our own and generate results (Perform).

When we learn, we move through all four parts of the learning process. Each part of the process connects directly to one of the questions learners seek to have answered: "Why," "What," "How," and "If."

In Engage, the Type One learners' favorite part of the learning process, we ask and answer, "Why."

In Share, the Type Two learners' favorite part of the learning process, we ask and answer, "What."

In Practice, the Type Three learners' favorite part of the learning process, we ask and answer, "How."

In Perform, the Type Four learners' favorite part of the learning process, we ask and answer, "If."

For real learning transfer to take place, all four parts of the Learning Cycle must be addressed. We do this by focusing on answering the four core questions. These questions form the connection between the learning style and the questions the learners are asking and answering. Notice how the answering of these questions leads the learner through the complete learning process.

> "Questions are the creative acts of intelligence."
> —Frank King

Type One learners ask "Why."

- Why is this important? To my work? To others?
- Why should I pay attention to this?
- Why is it of value?
- Why will I need to address this in my work?

Type Two learners ask "What."

- What do the experts think about this?
- What does the information show?
- What information is available to me?
- What are the identifiable patterns or trends?
- What data exists that supports this theory?

Type Three learners ask "How."

- How does this work?
- How can I use this in my job?
- How will incorporating this into my life help me?

Type Four learners ask "If."

- What if this is really true?
- What if I used this differently?

Asking Type One or Two learners to share their thoughts with the rest of the group can be uncomfortable if the learners have not had enough time to reflect and process. Instead of calling on a Type One or Two learner, ask for input from the group or ask someone whom you have already identified as a strong Type Three or Four learner.

- If I did this, what might happen?
- What if there are even more possibilities?

> "The important thing is not to stop questioning."
> —Albert Einstein

Let's take a look at an example of how questions drive the learning process:

Engage by answering "Why?"

Think about learning to ride a bike. Before learning to ride, you first had to want to learn. Maybe your brother had a bike you admired, or maybe you just wanted to be able to go someplace by yourself. When the reason you wanted to learn to ride, the **why**, became important enough to you, you were ready to learn. You became **engaged** in the idea of riding a bike.

Share by answering "What?"

You quickly found out **what** you needed to know. What are the important things you need to know about bike riding? What can you learn from watching others? What can your brother teach you? You listened to what others, the experts, had to **share** about riding a bike.

Practice by answering "How?"

Armed with this information, you had to learn **how** to do it yourself. You got on the bike with your dad holding the back of your seat, and then suddenly he let go. You **practiced** doing it, just the way he told you.

Perform by answering "If?"

No matter how much people told you about bike riding, it was not the same as doing it your way. That is when you really learned—when you did it your own quirky way. "**If** I rode

When you are facilitating activities, be conscious that the Type Three and Four learners will move into an activity before you have finished the directions. Be clear and concise when giving directions so you create clarity for those who need more structure, and be quick enough to keep everyone's attention.

> "There are many truths of which the full meaning cannot be realized until personal experience has brought it home."
>
> —John Stuart Mills

with only one hand, bounced off curbs, or only rode on one wheel, what would happen?" When you began to ask these questions, you had truly learned how to ride a bike. You **performed** your own version of riding a bike.

As you learned how to ride a bike, you traveled the Learning Cycle, as shown in figure 2-1, by answering the four questions: "Why?" "What?" "How?" and "If?"

The 4MAT Model for Training Design

Using these four questions as a foundation, you have the design format for any training design. Use the Learning Cycle as a template for designing learning strategies that mirror the way learning happens. It is as simple as asking yourself the following:

Figure 2-1. Learning to ride a bike.

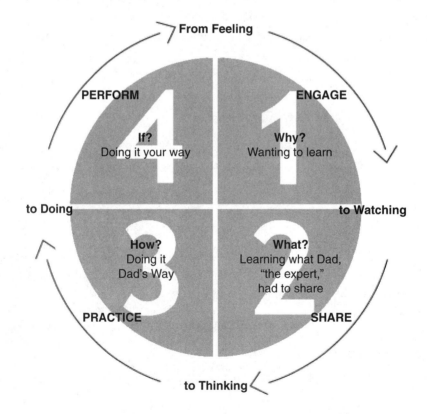

Figure 2-2. The Learning Cycle

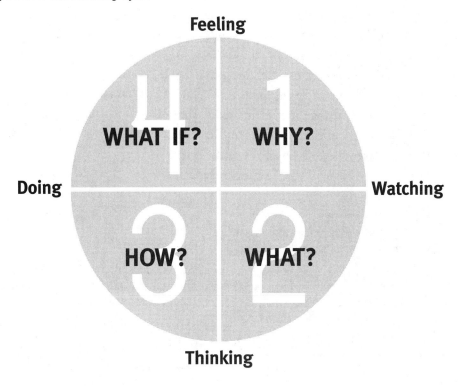

- Why do my learners need to know this?
- What is it that I am teaching them?
- How will they use it in their lives?
- If I am successful, what will they become as a result?

Notice how the 4MAT Model is a framework for designing any kind of training, from learning to ride a bike, to mastering a language, to becoming skilled in a new job. The 4MAT Model frames the learning process both for the learners (who must be personally engaged, understand the shared knowledge, take part in rigorous practice, and perform the learning) and the trainer (who must engage, instruct, facilitate practice, and assess performance).

By designing activities that encourage the learners to explore and answer these four questions, as figure 2-2 shows, you will engage all learner types and facilitate effective learning.

Your Success as a Trainer

When you use the 4MAT Model, you create engaging and transformative learning because you

- start with what the learners already know internally—their memory, their existing knowledge and connection to their own experiences—and move them to personalized uses of the learning in the external, real world
- create a balance between the learners' receiving and producing: in the first two parts of the Learning Cycle, Engage and Share, the learners receive through listening and sharing group perceptions and focusing on the knowledge and information available; in the final two parts of the Learning Cycle, Practice and Perform, the learners produce with hands-on skills practice and adaptation of the learning to personal needs
- engage every learner by addressing every part of the learning process.

> Only hand out materials when you are ready for the learners to begin working on them or reading them. If there is more lecture or direction that needs to be delivered before the handouts are used, do this before handing the materials out. Otherwise, the doing learners, the Type Three and Four learners, will begin the activity and tune out your directions.

The challenge in being an effective—even great—trainer is figuring out how to manage the needs of different types of learners as you move through the Learning Cycle. The trick is to move back and forth between the opposites of feeling and thinking and watching and doing. And the whole time you are doing this, be conscious that while one camp is comfortable, the other is not. The most effective way to do this is to consciously move through all four parts of the Learning Cycle. This is where stretching from your preferred way of learning becomes critical.

Most trainers find that they train most effectively in their preferred part of the Learning Cycle. Look at the type of activities trainers create and facilitate in each part of the Learning Cycle. Which do you find most comfortable?

What Does a Trainer Do in Each Part of the Learning Process?

The purpose of each part of the Learning Cycle is different. Table 2-1 shows what the trainer is looking for from the learners.

Engage: Engage the learners by connecting the content to their personal lives—their concerns, experiences, and needs. Stories, sharing, dialogue, and exploration are fundamental to this part of the learning process.

Table 2-1. The Learning Cycle goals.

Part of the Learning Cycle	Trainers Look for...	What the Learner Is Doing . . .
Engage 1 Engage	Reaction • interest and engagement • excitement, deep sharing, and frequency of questions	• reflecting • presentations of similarities or differences in experiences • engagement and deep, meaningful sharing
Share 2 Share	Learning • ability to understand the big idea and the relationship of the topics • demonstration of understanding through well-considered questions, visuals, or presentations	• review of key points and insights • creation of a mindmap or visual organizer that summarizes the learning • sharing of "aha's" and insights to flipcharts labeled with key points
Practice 3 Practice	Transfer • ability to demonstrate application in real-world, hands-on practice • integrating the information into their own work or personal lives	• demonstrations of application of the information • completion of worksheets or group review exercises • participation in game show-style activities that review key points • creation of cheat sheets, highlighting application of key points
Perform 4 Perform	Results • adaptation of information • demonstration of insights centered around implementation • commitment to application of the information	• display of portfolios that include examples of learner application of the information • presentations of material • feedback from coaches or team leaders • improvement in performance directly linked to skills learned

Share: Share the content, what the experts have to say on the subject. Lecture, video, expert presenters, presentations, and research are all appropriate for this part of the learning process.

Practice: Practice the skills and ideas you presented in Share. Hands-on activities such as simulations, role plays, field work, and case studies are taking place in this part of the learning process.

Perform: Perform the skills learned. The learners take ownership and determine how to use this information to produce greater results. Refining practice, online portfolios, frontline implementation, and competency assessment all take place in this part of the learning process.

Typically, we find that

- Type One learners and trainers love the Engage part of the learning process: the dialogue, the stories, and the opportunity to explore meaningful issues
- Type Two learners and trainers love the Share part of the learning process: the organized delivery of content sourced from expert thinking
- Type Three learners and trainers love the Practice part of the learning process: the practical application of the content to real-world problems
- Type Four learners and trainers love the Perform part of the learning process: the editing of their own work and having the creative freedom to adapt the learning to their own lives.

What Happens When Parts of the Learning Cycle Are Missing?

You might ask, "Do I have to do all four parts? What if there is not enough time?" You probably don't have to look too far to find examples of trainings that miss major parts of the Learning Cycle. Most trainings answer the question, "What." Many trainings answer the question, "How."

The most powerful learning experiences start and end with the personal connections that are found in the "Why" and "If" questions answered in Engage and Perform. Without the connection that happens in Engage and Perform, the learners do not own the information. The likelihood of real transfer happening diminishes greatly without the personal connection that happens in the second half of the Learning Cycle. When you design learning to include all four parts of the Learning Cycle, the learners take greater ownership of the learning. Each part of the learning process adds its own value to the learning.

What happens when Engage is missing from a training?

The learners have no opportunity to attach personal meaning to the content. The learners must figure out how the content applies to their lives, if at all. The trainer ends up working harder to keep the learners engaged throughout the rest of the learning process. The Type One learners are most dissatisfied.

What happens when Share is missing from a training?

The learning experience lacks structure and meatiness. The learners may question the credibility of the trainer and of the content. The learners may be confused by lots of dialogue and activity with no apparent framework holding it all together. The learners may be entertained, but not educated. The Type Two learners are most dissatisfied.

What happens when Practice is missing from a training?

Even with the best delivery of Engage and Share, if there is no opportunity to practice the skill, the likelihood of transfer is slim. The Type Three learners are most dissatisfied.

What happens when Perform is missing from a training?

Without an opportunity to refine their practice and put their own spin on the information, the learners are less likely to transfer the learning to the real world. The trainer has no opportunity to evaluate the learners' adaptations of the content. The Type Four learners are most dissatisfied.

> "If you don't have the right amount of quality thinking in a complex growth company like ours, it is going to manifest itself in terms of marginalized discussions that rely on wrong inputs and unskilled questions. And that's what drags down business."
>
> —Andrea Jung

To effectively train learners, trainers need to address each part of the Learning Cycle. In the next chapter, you will learn more about what the learners and trainer are doing in each of these steps in a well-designed training.

Your Learning Workshop:
Stretching Your Training Design

Start by asking yourself what question(s) you focus on the most. Do you spend more time on the

- Why?—the content is meaningful and important
- What?—the experts have to say about the content
- How?—the content can be used in the real world
- If?—the learners adapted the content for their own use.

When you design or deliver training, what questions are you most focused on answering for your learners? Begin thinking about how you can balance your attention to these four questions.

When observing trainers, pay attention to how they move through the four questions. As you observe a training, take a blank piece of paper and draw two lines across the page, forming four quadrants (see figure 2-3). Label each quadrant with one of the four questions. Make notes about what activities the trainer uses that fit with each learner question. Notice any questions that have less emphasis.

Figure 2-3. The Four Questions.

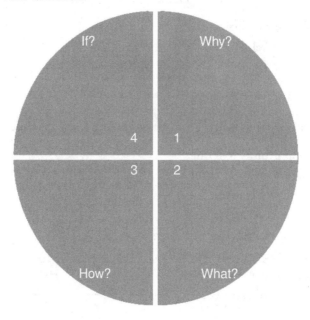

Chapter 3

The 4MAT Model
in the Classroom

$\longrightarrow$

As you incorporate the 4MAT Model into your training, you will be working in areas that are not your favorite places—places where you must stretch. You will find yourself dealing with the tension of both being yourself and stretching into new dimensions.

If you are a Type One learner, you understand the need for your participants to personalize the value of the material and you know this takes place best in discussions of shared perceptions, so you tend to have your participants linger there. Yet, you admit that you need to speed up your teaching strategies to get to the practical applications of the learning to get the results you want and so you stretch.

If you are a Type Two learner, the individualization that takes place as you move into the doing parts of the cycle will often seem like chaos to you and cause you to fear losing control. Yet, you are clear that learners must transfer what they learn into their own work lives, and this takes individual adaptations and so you stretch.

If you are a Type Three learner, you find the first part of the Learning Cycle, Engage, difficult. The motivation and personal connection activities are contrary to your strong need to get right to the doing of the learning. Yet, you admit intellectually that if you make sure your participants are with you emotionally before you move to action, you achieve more success and so you stretch.

If you are a Type Four learner, you want to hand the learning over to your participants because you know that is where all learning really takes hold. Your tendency is to do that too quickly. However, you admit that when you take the time to carefully structure the information delivery and the practice strategies, more successful transfer takes place and so you stretch.

Doing it all through the Learning Cycle keeps you in balance and on track.

The Learning Cycle

So far, we have identified the following key points:

- There are four types of learners, each with a preference for a particular part of the learning process.
- The learning process is a cycle that a trainer can divide into four parts: Engage, Share, Practice, and Perform.

> "Prior knowledge is a fact. Prior knowledge is persistent. Prior knowledge is the beginning of new knowledge."
>
> —James Zull

To design and deliver effective training, you will develop activities that move the learners through all four parts of the Learning Cycle. To prepare to do this, let's review what happens in each part of the Learning Cycle, as shown in table 3-1.

What Happens in the Learning Cycle?

Let's examine how the goals, climate, methods, success, and the trainer's role change as you move around the 4MAT Model.

ENGAGE: THE SEARCH FOR MEANING—WHY?

Your task in Engage is to create meaning, to draw on the learners' prior knowledge and experiences. You create an experience that helps the learners see the value of the information they are about to learn. When this is done effectively, the learners decide to commit to the learning experience and become engaged in the learning process.

The goal in Engage is personal connections—sharing of past experiences, insights, meanings brought into the discussions and conversations, experiences, and subjectivity honored and explored.

The learning climate needs to be easy, open, and inviting. The listening is focused on real dialogue.

The method is discussion.

- The group listens and shares.
- People are engaged on an emotional level.
- Attention is focused.

Table 3-1. Learning Cycle overview.

Four Parts of the Learning Cycle	Learning Goal	Learning Climate	Learning Method	You know it is ef
1 Engage — Engage (The question is "Why?")	Learners connect personally to the content being delivered.	Easy, open, and inviting; focuses on listening	Dialogue, discussion, and reflection	Learners are personal and insights r content. The l engaged and ready
2 Share — Share (The question is "What?")	Learners understand expert information related to the content.	Organized, focused, and reflective with an opportunity to ask questions	Lecture and interactive discussion on the content	Learners are noting, and que They are questions and better underst ideas.
3 Practice — Practice (The question is "How?")	Learners practice what they learned from the experts.	Active with a focus on hands-on, real-world application	Learner demonstration and coaching	Learners are practicing new figuring out informatio
4 Perform — Perform (The question is "If?")	Learners refine their own work and adapt the content for use in their work and life situations.	Dynamic, open-ended, challenging, and focused on future implementation and innovation	Learner implementation and assessment	Learners are own pract adapting the their own us

- There is an eagerness to learn.
- Diverse perceptions are discussed.
- There is a high level of listening.
- There is honest conversation and discussion.

The trainer is a motivator.

This first part of the learning process forms the foundation for the learning. This is where people live—their issues, concerns, viewpoints, mental models, beliefs, and views of the world. When you draw on the learner's experiences first, you are valuing them and helping them forge their own connections to the learning. When you effectively lead this part of the learning process, the learners are engaged and ready to learn.

In Engage, the learner is motivated and engaged:

- identifying needs
- clarifying purpose
- connecting meaning
- addressing people issues
- relating information to people's needs
- listening actively
- creating energy for focus.

The first step in any learning process is establishing a relationship to what we already know—some fundamental understanding that we already grasp. The more personal the connection is, the more valuable the information, and the assimilation of learning will ease.

When you are emotionally engaged in learning, you retain what you learn. That is why emotionally charged experiences stick with us. We remember moments of joy and pain in great detail.

It is no different in our work. When we are personally engaged in our work, we invest more emotion in the process, adding meaning to it. As a trainer, you must establish meaning.

Every experience, every report, every newspaper article, every email, every meeting is an opportunity to make meaning. We ask ourselves, "What does this mean?" "How does it relate to what I know?" "What do I need to do with this?" "What can be learned here?"

> "Dialogue is at the root of the learning process."
> —Asa Hilliard

"How can I make it work for me?" "Is this important?" and "Do I need to invest mental or physical energy in this?"

Each of us determines how much of our energy to invest based on the significance of the content. We ask ourselves, "What does this mean for me?" We connect new information and experiences to personal needs or desires.

Connect what you are about to teach to what is important to your group. Identify how the learning will affect them. Help them find their own meaning. This is the key to engaging the learners.

Engage is effective when the learners are engaged at the personal level.

SHARE: THE SEARCH FOR INFORMATION—WHAT?

The trainer's task in part two of the Learning Cycle, Share, is to organize the content to deliver key information and ideas. The trainer delivers expert knowledge by enabling learners to visualize and make connections. The learning must be organized conceptually. The content must be delivered in a structured manner that illustrates the relationship between topics.

The most effective way to structure content is by identifying core concepts that simply express the bigger idea that holds together related topics. For instance, the concept of win-win might be a concept you use to structure content focused on conflict resolution.

Some examples of core concepts are

- leadership development content might be structured around concepts such as authenticity, integrity, alignment, or potential
- stress management content might be structured around concepts such as balance, wellness, tension, or perception
- customer service content might be structured around concepts such as relationships, loyalty, managing expectations, or consistency.

How you present the major concepts that make up the material is the secret of Share. You must understand how the content all fits together to do this well.

The goal in Share is understanding—expert knowledge is explored; the key facts are explained and connected to the big ideas. The material is organized so that the learners can classify and compare the critical details.

The learning climate needs to be thoughtful. People reflect and think out loud. There is real focus.

> "Thinking isolates events, understanding them interconnects them. Understanding is structure, for it means establishing relationship between events."
> —Buckminster Fuller

The method is lecture.

- The group is focused on clarification.
- Past knowledge is under consideration.
- Important information is being discussed.
- The material is specific and concise.
- The details relate.
- The learners are establishing relationships.
- They are recording.
- They get the big idea, the underlying structure.

The trainer is a deliverer of expert knowledge and information.

Here in this second learning stage, your learners are receivers. They listen to the voices of the experts. If Share has been done well, the learners will discuss the expert knowledge and relate it to their previous experiences and the discussion you designed in Engage. Whenever possible, the lecture is interactive.

In Share, the learners understand the content conceptually:

- enhancing clarity
- connecting images
- recognizing patterns
- organizing information into meaningful chunks
- exploring ideas and knowledge
- comparing and contrasting
- gaining knowledge expertise.

In Engage, the learners experienced the meaning of the content. Now, they are learning what the experts have to share. As a trainer, you must keep connecting the facts to the big idea. Share is looking at what already exists, consulting resources and benchmarks, visualizing, organizing, and absorbing information.

Share is the organization of meaning. Structure drives learning. Without a discernible structure in the information presentation, the learners will fumble around trying to figure out a way to organize it. What is the most important information? What concepts can we use to organize the details?

Share is effective when the learners are clear on the conceptual structure of the content and how the topics relate.

PRACTICE: THE SEARCH FOR USEFULNESS—HOW?

The trainer's task in Practice is to facilitate practice, experimentation, and tinkering. The learners must put the learning to use. Here you allow time for meaningful practice activities that will help the learners build their skills. You set up various ways they may choose to master the skills that flow directly from the knowledge.

> "If it isn't used, it isn't learned."
>
> —Aleksandr Luria

You use multiple tasks that take the learners through each aspect of the material.

The goal in Practice is problem solving—perfecting and practicing skills, trying things out to see how they work, experimenting, predicting, tinkering, testing, and mastering.

The learning climate is active. People are tinkering and experimenting.

The method is coaching.

- The group is practicing and problem solving.
- People are messing with ideas.
- People are trying things out.
- The learning moves from understanding to application and use.

The trainer is a coach.

In this third learning stage, the participants are taking over the learning. The trainer moves into the wings. Some trainers have difficulty switching roles from teaching to coaching. This is understandable, given our classroom histories of listening to teachers deliver the lectures and quietly responding in writing. Most of us grew up with very quiet classrooms. Yet, we now know that learners must take over the learning, first tentatively with their coach assisting, and then finally leading the learning process.

In Practice, the learners begin to practice and produce results:

- experimenting with new skills
- solving problems as they arise
- mastering new skills
- building competence
- experimenting with applications
- figuring out how things work
- making on-the-job applications.

Results happen in Practice. People solve problems, try out new ideas, innovate, and produce. This is where real work gets done. It is the place in the Learning Cycle where the learners move into action.

The shift from Share to Practice is the shift from ideas to application. Many trainers fall short here. The learners must practice and extend skills into the work setting. Practice is where the training payoff begins.

Bernice on the Need for Practice

I did not realize how difficult my teaching style was, not only for the Type Three learners, who relish step-by-step instructions initially to get to mastery, but also for all the learners who felt I was too open-ended with my multiple options.

One day John came to see me. John was a Type Three learner, and I loved his straight-forwardness and common sense. We were good friends.

"Dr. McCarthy," he said, "we cannot figure out exactly what it is you want us to do. You have all these great ideas, and most of us love to listen to you talk about them, but when it comes to getting the job done and getting through this, we really need more help. Just telling us to create something with the learning is not my idea of a structured task I can grab on to."

I now understand the practice part of implementation, the feedback, and the need for learners to refine their own adaptations. That is what makes successful training transfer. You can have the most motivating beginning, with elegant, authentic dialogue in Engage, followed by a beautiful presentation that would make any trainer proud, but if you do not create the implementation steps, with a solid coaching process monitored and measured, learning will not occur. The Type Three learners have taught me a lot.

Training without active participation means learning does not happen. The learners may be interested or even inspired, but without practice, they will not be able to transfer the learning.

Your job as a trainer is to answer, "What do people need to be able to do after the training is complete?" Answering this question well is the key to designing a great Practice experience.

Practice is effective when the learners are taking the lead, practicing new skills, and figuring out how to apply the learning.

PERFORM: THE SEARCH FOR POSSIBILITIES—IF?

4 Perform

The trainer's task in Perform is to help the learners transfer the learning into their work. Now the learners are ready to perform, using their new skills with an adaptation that suits their needs. In this part of the Learning Cycle, the trainer and the learners set up an assessment plan to measure the implementation. This is where the learners integrate new knowledge and the skills back into their own lives.

The goal in Perform is adapting, refining, re-working, re-presenting, integrating, evaluating progress, and, most of all, performing.

The learning climate is dynamic, open-ended, renewing, and challenging. The participants are asking better questions.

The method is learner implementation and assessment.

> "Anyone who has begun to think places a portion of the world in jeopardy."
> —John Dewey

- The group is acting and using.
- They are integrating learning.
- People are taking their knowledge in new directions.
- The group is enhancing their work lives.

The trainer is a supportive evaluator and a cheerleader.

This is the final learning stage, where transfer happens, the goal of all teaching and training. The trainer becomes unnecessary.

In Perform, the learners refine skills and adapt learning in new ways:

- refining
- seeing new possibilities
- envisioning
- sharing new extensions of knowledge
- asking, "How could we do this better?"
- giving and receiving feedback
- following up on performance
- making new connections
- finding new questions
- celebrating success.

In Perform, the learners perform, evaluate, and reflect on their performances. This is where learning comes together.

> "If they cannot say, 'I did it myself,' they are lost to us."
> —James Zull

As the learners complete the Learning Cycle in Perform, they step into the heart of continuous improvement. Innovation lives here. New life is breathed into processes; vision is renewed.

At the individual level, learners reflect on their own performances and engage in feedback. It is where they begin to see new possibilities in their work and personal lives, generating ideas for improving processes, products, and procedures.

A learning environment that honors the Perform part of the Learning Cycle is an environment that leverages learning. The learners realize their potential and assess how they are doing. They take ownership of the learning; it becomes theirs, and they carry it with them.

Perform is effective when the learners are demonstrating new skills and the ability to assess performance and identify areas for continuous improvement.

Your Style and Your Training

Your style can make a difference in how you train, even when you are familiar with the theory and have fluid expertise in the Learning Cycle.

Type One Learners as Trainers

Your own learning style can make a difference in how you plan and execute your training. Pay attention to how your strengths and weaknesses as a learner affect your training. Examine your training strengths and weaknesses resulting from your "Oneness." You shine in Quadrant One and probably need to work on your Quadrant Three strategies.

YOUR SUCCESS IN ENGAGE

Engage is your place to shine. Nobody does this better than you. And Engage is the hardest quadrant to do well. You really understand how people need to connect, and you create wonderful beginnings to engage them. Remember though, the Type One learners in your group love to ramble on, and, if allowed, they could take you away from your content goals. Be sure you maintain coherence between the opening experience, the dialogue in Engage, and the content to be presented in Share. Always connect your beginning activities with the content to be learned. The 4MAT Model will support you in doing this.

YOUR SUCCESS IN SHARE

You do pretty well here, also. You have a good command of the content, and you stay on track. You present the material in an orderly fashion. Because talking is really something Type One people love to do, be careful of your tendency to lecture too long. While you are having a kinesthetic experience up front, the Type Three and Four learners tend to become impatient with sitting and listening.

Your Success in Practice

You organize good practice sessions. You need to make sure you include monitoring the back-to-work usefulness of the workshop content for successful transfer.

Your Success in Perform

You are good with people, but the Type Four learners tend to make you nervous. They are too quick to try things when you are still explaining. Try to be more open with their enthusiasm, and trust them to go off on their own. Keep after them for results after the training is finished.

Type Two Learners as Trainers

Examine your training strengths and weaknesses resulting from your Twoness. You shine in Quadrant Two and probably need to work on your Quadrant Four strategies.

Your Success in Engage

You do a fine job of making sure the objectives of the training are clear, but you tend to do too much telling. You may need to work on creating settings and experiences where the explanation of the objectives becomes part of a dialogue. You do not have to water down your objectives to accomplish this; on the contrary, your learning purposes will be more accepted and your learners more engaged if you begin with dialogue.

Your Success in Share

You do this well. You are a good lecturer. You know your material, and you present it in an organized way. Your learners really appreciate this. The only caveat is that you do not drown your learners in details. Create activities where they can discover some of the important details on their own during Practice, and be sure to connect details to the big idea. Try an interactive lecture where you stop along the way to allow reaction and feedback.

Your Success in Practice

You do this well; your love for details and your patience in helping learners get it right works. Watch out for overkill on practice. Move your reluctant learners forcefully into on-the-job adaptations.

Your Success in Perform

You are skilled at helping learners refine their adaptations, but not as open to their originality and risk-taking tendencies. Stay with them for transfer of the learning into their everyday work, even though they may not use the learning in exactly the ways you intended.

Type Three Learners as Trainers

Examine your training strengths and weaknesses resulting from your Threeness. You shine in Quadrant Three and probably need to work on your Quadrant One strategies.

Your Success in Engage

This is not really your strong suit. Group learning is difficult for you, yet that is exactly what has to happen in this part. You need to create an experience that is analogous to the content you will be teaching in Share. Have learners share their perceptions before you begin the trainer-directed part of the workshop so they are engaged before you begin lecturing.

Your Success in Share

You do fine here. You are not fond of lecturing, but you do it well enough. Your lectures usually cut right to the chase. Work on adding more life to them with anecdotes, stories, and interactive dialogues. You might try stopping at key points in a lecture and ask pertinent, even controversial questions.

Your Success in Practice

You are excellent here. You are patient and down-to-earth. You structure even the most complicated tasks for elegant, sequenced small bites, making it easy for your learners to succeed. And you keep connecting the practice to how to use the learning back on their jobs, the necessary boost to transfer.

Your Success in Perform

You are pretty good here, also. Your organization skills usually include valuable assessment strategies. You do, however, tend to discourage creative applications in favor of by-the-book uses. Work on being more open to allowing, even encouraging, your learners to create unusual ways of transferring the learning to their lives.

Bernice on Fourness Without Twoness

My Type Four learning style has stood me in good stead all of my life, but I needed a great teacher to convince me it just wasn't enough. When I entered the doctoral program at Northwestern, Bill Hazard was assigned to be my advisor. He was one of the best teachers and coaches I have ever had, and he was tough. But along with the toughness, he convinced me at our first meeting that he believed in me. And that belief made a great difference in what followed.

After I handed in my first assignment, he returned it covered in red ink. If it had been a living creature, it surely would have bled to death. Everywhere I used words without explanation, his red ink appeared. I seemed to have expected the world to know my meanings without the bother of any tiresome explanations. Well, he did not agree. He hit on many of my words and phrases asking, "Exactly, what do you mean by this?" "Is this the correct meaning for this word?" or "Have you made up your own definition?" The paper was filled with such questions and admonitions. A sober and chastened student revised the work and returned it to him.

For the remainder of my time at Northwestern, Bill Hazard was my most outspoken critic. As I look back, I realize I never could have written my first book without the discipline he taught me. He moved me from a superficial Four to a disciplined person who learned to check the research, use the dictionary frequently (especially the section on word origins), and grow in my ability to honor and respect my critics.

We all need to go to our opposite places on the natural cycle to achieve optimum growth. To remain only comfortable in one style is to deny our potential. If we are lucky enough, we will meet one or two teachers along the way who insist that we do. Blessings on those teachers.

In special memory of Bill Hazard.

Type Four Learners as Trainers

Examine your training strengths and weaknesses resulting from your Fourness.

YOUR SUCCESS IN ENGAGE

You do okay in Engage because you are interested in how people perceive things. Your only problem is that you have little patience with the folks who need to talk out their feelings in the kind of time you consider too long. Work on giving your participants enough time to become really engaged with the content.

YOUR SUCCESS IN SHARE

You certainly know the theory. You need to be sure you spend the time necessary in this part of the Learning Cycle, being clear as you explain the information. Your tendency is to put it out there and let people play with it themselves. Your love of theory is a wandering love, and you move through many connections when you are fascinated with knowledge. Sometimes, your learners are puzzled by that and can become downright discouraged. They begin to fear that they will never see all the ramifications and connections that you see.

YOUR SUCCESS IN PRACTICE

You tend to underestimate the importance of this part of the Learning Cycle. One of your traits, both for good and ill, is your speed. You are accustomed to doing things quickly, on your own, and with little help. So you are not at all sure why people need a trainer to hold their hands. You may even find it surprising that people often need detailed, step-by-step practice with something you were able to grasp right away. Can't they just get going and figure it out themselves? Be sure you create practice activities that cover all the important steps. Take the time to go back if some of the learners need more help.

YOUR SUCCESS IN PERFORM

Here you are a star. You dream up wonderful projects, impart great enthusiasm, and inspire the creative folks with lots of ideas. You need to make sure assessment happens so results will be clear. You need carefully crafted evaluations of implementation transfer for this, and that is a stretch for you.

To effectively design a training, you must not only know the type of trainer and learner you are, but also know the steps to implement the most effective and lasting training, which will be explored in the next chapter.

Your Learning Workshop:
Stretching Your Evaluation of Past Workshops

Assess your past training experiences. Pay special attention to your favorite ways of conducting training. What strategies seem to work well for you? What quadrants do they favor? Go over past trainings that were less than what you wanted. Examine the reasons in light of your understanding of the 4MAT Model. Focus on certain learners in your training you did not seem to reach, and ask yourself if you spent enough time in the quadrants they needed.

Chapter 4

Great Training Design: The Steps of the Learning Cycle

The Learning Cycle involves moving through four distinct phases, each with a focus on a unique question. If you think of learning as the process of answering these four questions, the training design process is simplified:

- Why do I want to learn this?
- What exactly am I learning?
- How will I use this in my life?
- What new possibilities will this learning create?

The 4MAT Model is a framework that takes learners through the Learning Cycle for a complete learning experience. It is a simple, common sense teaching and training adaptation of what we know about how people learn. Each of the four quadrants of the Learning Cycle has two key steps. These steps are the result of brain research on the hemisphericity divisions of left mode and right mode:

- Left Mode: Operates out of analysis; uses language, abstracts, and experiences; has number sense and is sequential
- Right Mode: Operates out of being, comprehends images, seeks patterns, creates metaphors, and is simultaneous.

We use the terms synthesis for the right mode and analysis for the left mode (figure 4-1). Each quadrant is designed to move the learners back and forth, between right and left mode, between synthesis and analysis.

Figure 4-1. Hemiphericity divisions.

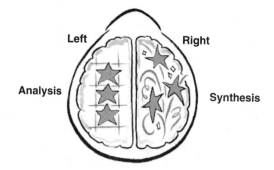

Engage (favorite part of the Type One learners)

- Step 1: We learn from our experiences and from who and where we are. We become personally involved (synthesis).
- Step 2: We share our perceptions and ideas about these experiences, exploring our thinking, both within ourselves and often in dialogue (analysis).

> Synthesis is the composition or combination of parts or elements so as to form a whole, the combining of often diverse conceptions into a coherent whole.

Share (favorite part of the Type Two learners)

- Step 3: We understand conceptually, picture how it all fits together (synthesis).
- Step 4: We comprehend the underlying concepts and how they connect all the details (analysis).

Practice (favorite part of the Type Three learners)

- Step 5: We examine the steps and the parts to practice with supportive coaching (analysis).
- Step 6: We apply the learning to real-life problem solving (synthesis).

> Analysis is the separation of a whole into its component parts, an examination of a complex, its elements, and their relations; it is a method of resolving complex expressions into simpler ones.

Figure 4-2. Eight steps of learning.

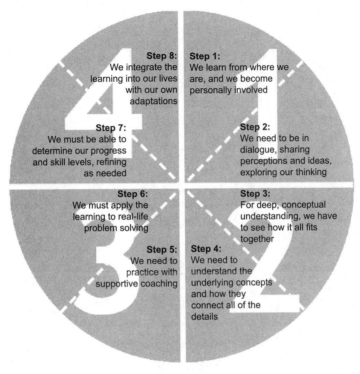

 Perform (favorite part of the Type Four learners)

- Step 7: We evaluate our progress and skill levels, refining and editing as needed (analysis).
- Step 8: We integrate the learning into our lives with our own adaptations (synthesis).

Now, look at the eight steps of learning overlaid on the 4MAT Model, as shown in figure 4-2.

These eight steps form the basis for the 4MAT Model. To design effective training, you will use these eight steps to determine how best to deliver content. By using all eight steps, you will effectively address key brain concepts:

- *perceptions and connections*—creating an opportunity for the learners to explore what they already know about the content and connect the meaning to their personal lives

> "We shall not cease from exploration, and the end of all our exploring will be to arrive where we started and know the place for the first time."
>
> —T. S. Eliot

Figure 4-3. Eight steps in the 4MAT Model.

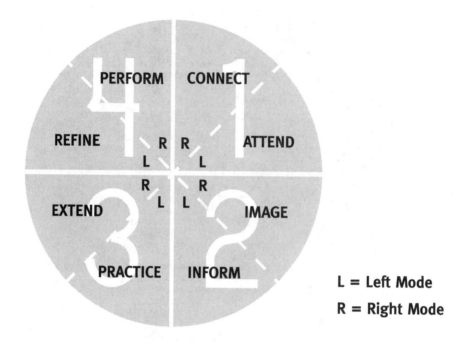

- *reflections and actions*—creating a balance in the learning between reflecting on the ideas and acting on the ideas
- *language and images*—using both words and graphic organizers to enhance understanding and retention
- *big ideas and details (wholes and parts)*—sharing the big picture and breaking down the details to enhance understanding; constantly weaving new information back to the core idea
- *ladders and networks*—outlining the steps and creating relationships.

Most important, you will ensure that you are addressing the needs of every learner by designing learning that appeals to all four learning styles.

The Eight Steps of the 4MAT Model

As you can see, the 4MAT Model addresses the key brain concepts by leading the learners through the eight steps shown in figure 4-3. As we explore the eight steps further in this chapter, notice how each step addresses key brain concepts.

Engage: Steps 1 and 2

In Engage, you will create an opportunity for the learners to explore the personal meaning of the content and reflect on their own experiences.

STEP 1: CONNECT

Co (with) + nectere (to bind)

What the learners are doing:

- establishing relationship between content and how it connects to their lives
- experiencing something, rather than being told about something
- connecting to the heart of the content
- reflecting and sharing
- becoming intrigued and engaged.

What the trainer is doing:

- connecting the learners directly to the concept in a personal way
- capturing the learners' attention by initiating a group problem-solving activity before delivery of instruction
- beginning with a situation that is familiar and builds on what the learners already know
- constructing a learning experience or simulation that generates diverse response and personal discussions
- eliciting meaningful dialogue
- asking the learners to reflect on their own experiences and share their insights.

STEP 2: ATTEND

Ad (to, toward) + tendere (to stretch)

What the learners are doing:

- analyzing what just happened in Connect
- attending to the experiences and the perceptions of their colleagues
- noticing the similarities and differences in experiences
- discussing what really happened
- sharing with real dialogue.

What the trainer is doing:

- guiding the learners to reflect on the experience
- encouraging the learners to share personal perceptions and beliefs

- summarizing and reviewing similarities and differences
- establishing a positive attitude toward the diverse perceptions and beliefs of the group
- connecting with the learners at a personal level.

Share: Steps 3 and 4

In Share, you will share the content with learning, both visually and nonvisually.

STEP 3: IMAGE

Imaginen (to form a mental picture)

What the learners are doing:

- visualizing or picturing the concept before hearing it in a lecture
- seeing the bigger picture of the content about to be delivered.

What the trainer is doing:

- using another medium (neither reading nor writing) to connect the learners to the concept (visual arts, music, movement, etc.)
- involving the learners in reflection, blending the emotional and the cognitive
- transforming the concept to be taught into an image or experience—a sneak preview for the learners
- deepening the connection between the expert knowledge and the learners' work
- providing a metaview for the learners to view the concept more broadly
- creating opportunity for the learners to see the bigger picture of the concept.

STEP 4: INFORM

In (in, into) + form (form, shape, mold)

What the learners are doing:

- receiving information
- taking notes
- asking questions
- discussing relevant points.

What the trainer is doing:

- sharing information and knowledge
- delivering lecture

- emphasizing the most significant points in an organized way
- drawing attention to important, discrete details
- using a variety of delivery systems: interactive lecture, readings, expert speakers, visuals, and live demonstrations.

Practice: Steps 5 and 6

In Practice, you will create an opportunity for the learners to apply the knowledge and skills learned to their real-life situations.

STEP 5: PRACTICE

Praktikos (capable of being used)

What the learners are doing:

- practicing or demonstrating their understanding of the expert knowledge shared in Inform
- engaging in activities that allow an opportunity to practice using the information learned in Inform.

What the trainer is doing:

- providing hands-on activities for practice and mastery
- checking for understanding of concepts and skills with course materials: worksheets, problems, simulations, and review exercises
- helping learners to organize their possible adaptations
- assisting learners in finding needed resources
- determining if there is a need to revisit any important information before moving forward.

STEP 6: EXTEND

Ex (out of) + tendere (to stretch)

What the learners are doing:

- experimenting with their new knowledge and skills
- applying the information in a way that is relevant to how it will be used in the real world
- practicing how they will apply the information in their own lives.

What the trainer is doing:

- setting up situations where the learners use the information in a situation that is highly relevant to their work or personal lives
- giving the learners the opportunity to work with ideas and design open-ended explorations of the concept
- providing options for the learners to create demonstrations or extensions of learning
- allowing the learners to determine how their work will be evaluated
- defining their own criteria for assessment.

Perform: Steps 7 and 8

In Perform, you will create an opportunity for the learners to create their own adaptations of the learning and take the learning into their own work and life situations.

STEP 7: REFINE

Re (again) + fin (the end, limit, boundary)

What the learners are doing:

- taking ownership of the information and skills
- assessing their progress and performance
- refining their practice
- assessing their application of the information practiced in Steps 5 and 6.

What the trainer is doing:

- giving guidance and feedback
- encouraging the learners to be responsible for their own learning
- asking the learners to coach their own and others' applications of the information, as shared in Extend
- helping the learners to refine their new adaptations of learning to determine its relevance and originality
- maintaining high expectations for completion of the new demonstrations of learning
- helping possible missteps become learning opportunities.

> "Our only recourse is to begin with what the learner brings ... so often we conceive of teaching as starting with our own knowledge rather than that of the learner."
>
> —James Zull

46

STEP 8: PERFORM
Per (through) + form (form, shape, mold)

What the learners are doing:

- celebrating and performing
- demonstrating an original application of the learning that has high relevance to their work or personal lives.

What the trainer is doing:

- facilitating learning and sharing among learners
- making individual learning available to the larger group
- creating opportunities for continuing learning and innovation
- setting up follow-up and feedback loops
- applying measurements to the learning
- giving quality feedback
- establishing an atmosphere that celebrates learning
- eliciting commitment to active implementation of the learning.

More Help with Engage

For learning to begin, the learners have to connect what they already know to the content being learned. Yet, teaching or training tends to be primarily telling. The dialogue part of training is supposed to happen after we have given the learners enough knowledge so that they can carry on some kind of dialogue. The supposition has always been, our learners do not know the content or else why would we be training them?

What's Already There?

It's likely that there are already elements of Engage in your training design. Do you have an activity designed to engage learners at the feeling level? Do you ask them to consider the "Why" of your content? For example, do you ask, "Why is this important to know"? Do you set them up with a situation that intrigues and leaves them eager for content to come?

You may be wondering what the difference is between an Engage activity and an icebreaker. Icebreakers are designed to get the group warmed up and familiar with one another. A powerful Engage activity does this and, at the same time, focuses the learners on the bigger idea of the content. An effective Engage activity has the learners explore what they already know and understand about the underlying concept of the content they are about to learn.

Note: If an activity involves the trainer telling, it probably does not belong in the Engage part of the Learning Cycle.

What Should You Think About?

- Think experiential—something happens.
- Think of a lot of images lying about that can be chosen in silence, and then help the learners connect them to the concept.
- Think talk-story where learners relate past experiences around a concept.
- Think about the problems that are analogous to the skills you want them to master.
- Think about small, cooperative groups of learners.
- Think about the scenarios that could really take place.
- Think of the absence of something you are about to teach.
- Think music.
- Think process.
- Think right mode.
- Think about provoking discussion.
- Think about the learners sharing their stories related to the content.
- Think interactive.
- Think about how to relate the content to the learners' lives.
- Think about connecting to what is familiar.
- Think about the learners in every class that ask, "Why do I need to learn this?"

Examples of Engage Activities

- **Create a scenario.** The course is on attorney and client confidentiality. This is a law school unit designed to enhance awareness as to the serious nature of the promise of confidentiality between attorneys and their clients. The opening activity raised the issue on three levels, each level increasing the responsibility and personal injury issues. It was a very emotional activity because all of the law students dreamed of having one of their articles published in the law review, making their job offers at graduation much more lucrative and prestigious. A friend admits plagiarism of an article in order to make

> "Images are potentially malleable building blocks for creating larger ideas ... rich vehicles for meaning.... [T]hey invite grasping, handling, tinkering and building."
>
> —Chuck Paulus

appointment to the law review. The group must choose what they would do if (1) they were not involved, except as fellow students, (2) they were the editors of the law review, or (3) their article was not chosen because of the plagiarized article.

- **Create a simulation.** The course is on effective group decision making. Have small groups of learners participate in a survival game. The learners must choose 10 of 20 possible items to take with them on a deserted island.
- **Create a game.** The course is on the effect of body language and tone in presentation skills. One learner stands in the front of the room and is asked to share the statement, "There is enough ice cream" while conveying one of six emotions. The audience must determine which of the six emotions is being conveyed: frustration, anger, excitement, joy, disinterest, or boredom. The learner in the front of the room continues demonstrating until everyone in the audience agrees on the emotion being conveyed.

2 Share

More Help With Share

Share is where you, literally, share the key information. A good lecture is relatively short—less than 30 minutes. There are many ways to make your lecture lively and interactive. Be creative in sharing information. "Inform" definitely does not mean that you are talking the entire time.

What's Already There?

Think about what content you want to share. Videos, reading material, websites, and lectures by subject matter experts can all be included here.

What Should You Try?

- Try laughter and humor.
- Try demonstrations that clarify the content.
- Try images that illustrate the ideas, including magazine clippings, mindmaps, cartoons, movie clips, and visual organizers.
- Try practice tools learners can be practicing with while they hear the lecture.
- Try paying special attention to note taking, especially encouraging creative note taking.
- Try honoring questions as they arise.
- Try forming groups where people come up with the big question based on what they are hearing.
- Try encouraging listening, recording, analyzing, and questioning.

- Try thinking of ways the learners can present the information.
- Try having the learners read and summarize or research and report to the group.
- Try encouraging the learners to comment on their colleagues' responses before moving to another question.
- Try using open-ended questions to encourage dialogue.
- Try encouraging the learners to paraphrase.
- Try asking follow-up questions: "Why?" "Do you agree?" "Can you elaborate?" "Can you tell me more?" "Can you give an example?"
- Try providing thinking time after each question and after each response.
- Try playing devil's advocate.
- Try allowing time for the learners to develop their own questions.
- Try taking visual notes when acting as facilitator for class discussion.
- Try visually organizing the dialogue into themes.

Examples of Share Activities

- **Use the pass-the-folder discussion format.** This is a customer service workshop. Each small group gets a folder representing a different aspect of a customer service issue. Each group discusses the issue for a few minutes and records their contributions. The groups pass their folders to the next group, repeating the process until all groups have added their thoughts to each folder. At the end, each group reports on the folder they ended up with.
- **Create concepts.** This is an employee orientation. After lecturing for 20–30 minutes on company history and values, employees are asked to develop concept maps (visual organizers that illustrate big ideas). Have the learners share individual concept maps in groups, visually organizing the big ideas of the lecture. On a large piece of paper on the wall, the entire group combines its insights into one large concept map that represents the big ideas that the company stands for.
- **Look at hypotheticals.** This is a strategic planning session. For example, "If you were creating an organization that would compete with our company, what would be your three key competitive focuses?"

3
Practice

More Help with Practice

Part three of the Learning Cycle is where the learners practice the skills they will take back with them into the work setting.

What's Already There?

What activities do you normally include that allow the learners to demonstrate their application of the skill? Role plays, worksheets, and online quizzes are examples of common activities that fit well into this part of the training design.

What Should You Try?

- Try seeing how information works on the job.
- Try field trips to observe skills in action.
- Try interviews with customers, colleagues, or competitors.
- Try fieldwork or simulations.
- Try demonstrations.
- Try practice simulations of real-world applications.
- Try problem-solving sessions.
- Try worksheets, questions, and scenarios.
- Try allowing time for applying what people have learned.
- Try role playing.
- Try assigning projects that apply the skills learned.

Examples of Practice Activities

- **Create a scenario.** This is a training on effective coaching skills for managers. Learners are given scenarios dealing with common performance issues. The groups are asked to create a role play to show how an effective manager might best coach an employee.
- **Design a field trip.** This is a training on quality customer service standards. Using the customer service standards shared in the Inform part of the training design, the learners visit service locations and rate the service level using the standards provided.

4 Perform — More Help with Perform

Part four of the Learning Cycle is the part of the learning process where the learners refine their practice and create demonstrations of their learning. The learners step in, practice the content, and integrate the learning into their own work or personal lives.

What's Already There?

Think about how you normally assess the learners' grasp of the new learning. What are some ways the learners can demonstrate how well they have reached the learning objectives?

What Should You Try?

- Try having the learners refine their work from Practice.
- Try having the learners evaluate each other's work.
- Try having the learners create dialogue with others.
- Try having the learners celebrate the learning experience.
- Try having the learners move to the front and center.
- Try having the learners use game-show format reviews.
- Try having the learners present new integrations or adaptations.
- Try having the learners write reports or articles for sharing learning with the larger organization.
- Try having the learners share success stories.
- Try having the learners create new exhibitions of employee contributions or advancements.
- Try having the learners share different applications of the content.

Examples of Perform Activities

- **Develop a portfolio.** This is a training on leadership development. Leadership program candidates create portfolios that include project outcomes, a reflection journal on insights, video of presentations given, and a competency matrix of skills demonstrated at the conclusion of a 12-week leadership development program.
- **Write a story.** This is a training on corporate story telling. The learners, a senior-level leadership team, collectively write and share a corporate story that illustrates the core values of the organization. The story is then published in the corporate newsletter.

The Eight Steps of a Training

Let's take a look at what happens in each of the eight steps using the example of a workshop we designed for a client on conflict resolution.

Step 1: Connect

The design issue is always how to engage the learners. What opening should we use? What motivating, connecting activity, with an emotional charge, should we choose to begin with?

We chose the Learning Type Measure because we wanted the group members to experience how people see things differently, and this survey is a very powerful means of doing this. And seeing things differently is at the heart of most conflict resolution. Remember, the key to engaging the learners is connecting to what they already know and relating the content to their personal lives. When the learners assess their own styles, they immediately begin to relate to the information, at personal levels.

We followed the Learning Type Measure survey results with a discussion of the differences in learning styles:

- Type One learners: people people
- Type Two learners: data, statistics people
- Type Three learners: get-the-job-done people
- Type Four learners: take-a-risk people.

Note: This exercise is personally meaningful, engages people by starting with their experiences, and connects to the concept of diversity. This is what to look for in Step 1.

Step 2: Attend

We then moved to sharing perceptions about conflict. We initiated a discussion centered on four myths, one of which is, "Conflict is always negative." In small groups, the learners were asked to choose one of the four myths and recount an instance when the exact opposite of this was true. We were looking for personal experiences to debunk the myths. This worked extremely well.

Note: The learners have opportunities to dialogue about their perceptions. By introducing the four myths, we encouraged even deeper dialogue. Getting the learners to reflect on and share their own experiences of the information is the focus in Step 2.

Step 3: Image

We created an activity that connected the concept with the content. We introduced descriptions of four kinds of needs in conflict situations. We asked the learners to create visuals of how these four needs relate to each other in conflict situations.

Note: This activity has the learners think about diverse needs in a non-negative frame. The trainer has not lectured about diversity or needs but is asking the learners to imagine how these needs might be interrelated and could be used beneficially.

Step 4: Inform

We began to deliver the content. We began with a series of quotes on the underlying causes of human conflict and had the learners choose their favorites. Learners were asked to share their favorite quotes with the larger group.

Next, we lectured for 20 minutes on the four basic principles of effective conflict resolution. We ended with an overview of how to use the 4MAT Model as a framework for conflict resolution.

Note: The Inform part of the Learning Cycle does not need to be all lecture. We used quotes on conflict as a way to deliver the content in a more interesting way.

Step 5: Practice

We asked the learners to examine and manipulate research findings that indicate what does not work in a conflict situation. We asked the learners to match typical negative remarks with predicted outcomes. Next, each learner chose a partner to practice using feedback techniques that have been shown to work in managing conflict.

Note: This is a safe, first step in practicing new skills. First, the learners are matching the typical negative remarks, which bring all the mistakes people make into the open. Next, they practice what will work. This prepares the learners for putting the skills into action in the next step of the Learning Cycle.

Step 6: Extend

What task will take the learned skills back to the learners' workplace, transferring the learning into permanent behavior change?

We had learners from the same work teams choose a recent conflict in which they were involved. Using the 4MAT Model, each group examined the steps they had done well and identified the ones they could have done better. We assisted the groups in this task with a series of questions. For example, "The hallmark of a successful conflict resolution is an improvement of the relationships. Were relationships improved?"

Note: The learners are working on real-world problems. They are being asked to use the same skills that they practiced in the previous step in a real-world situation.

Step 7: Refine

The learners are refining the work practiced in Step 6. The goal is to have the learners assess the learning. The learners now examine the research on the three possible outcomes to conflict: unsatisfactory, neutral, and optimal. The key skills shared in Inform are reinforced. Learners answered the essential question from the beginning of the workshop: "Can conflict be productive and even transforming, and how and when?" This was followed by individual reflections on how they might have improved the outcome of the previous conflict example they shared.

Note: The learners are assessing their own skills. By sharing concrete criteria to evaluate outcomes, the learners have the opportunity to evaluate their own performances.

Step 8: Perform

The learners are integrating everything they have learned, preparing themselves to take the learning into their own lives. The learners were asked to complete the following statements regarding a conflict they were presently working on: "A positive for me in this conflict is…" "A positive for the other person is…" "A positive for the relationship is…."

The learners then chose partners and shared their statements. A date was set for a follow-up session with the group. Each group committed to reviewing results, following up on key insights, and discussing alternate uses of the framework. Evaluation forms were then completed.

Note: The learners will explore their understanding of conflict as a productive and essential process by stating the positive aspects of conflict. By scheduling a follow-up session, the trainer encourages immediate use of these new skills.

In the next chapter you will explore a step-by-step guide in how to use the 4MAT Model to create your own training designs.

Your Learning Workshop:
Stretching into the Eight Steps

Review a training design you have created. Using the wheel in figure 4-4, make notes of the steps you incorporated into your design. Are there any steps missing? Would you make any changes to the flow of your training design using the eight steps?

Figure 4-4. Eight steps in the 4MAT Model.

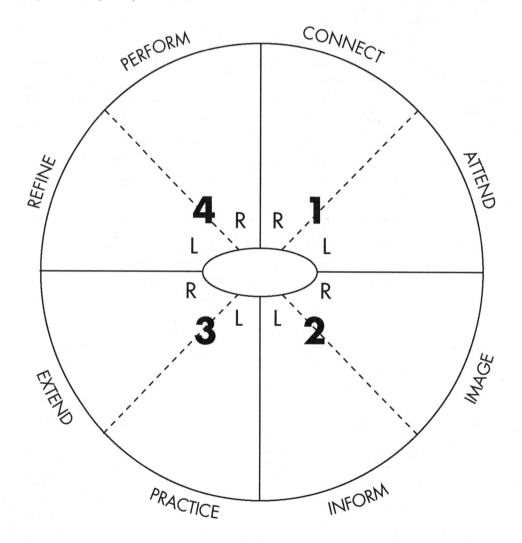

Chapter 5

The 4MAT Model
Lesson Plan

In this chapter, you will find a guide to help you design your own training plans. Before you begin filling in your 4MAT training design wheel, you will need to do the following:

- Define the learner outcomes in terms of both content and skills.
- Mindmap the content, looking for how the content is connected.
- Define the concept.

Step 1: Define the Learner Outcomes

You must be clear about the knowledge and skills you want your learners to master before you begin to create your training design. Define the results of the training. You can begin by asking the following questions:

- What will the learners know and be able to do better?
- How will the learners connect these ideas to their work lives and, in some cases, to their personal lives?
- What new skills will the learners have, and what will these skills give them access to?
- How will the learners demonstrate what they learn?

Answering the question, "How will the learners demonstrate what they will learn?" will lead you to describing the Perform step of your 4MAT Model. In Perform, you will ask the learners to demonstrate their achievement of the learning objective. Keep

> "A wonderful harmony arises from joining together the seemingly unconnected."
>
> —Heraclitus

in mind that this step should be an integral part of the final assessment and evaluation of the effectiveness of the learning.

Think about how the learners can synthesize all the knowledge and skills gained in the training. For example, in an eight-week leadership development program, you might ask the learners to complete a competency portfolio that includes examples, or proof of learning, of all the key skills learned. Depending on the content, the required examples of learning could include videotape presentations, reflections on coaching conversations with team members, or an action plan for continued development of strengths. An example such as this is effective because it integrates all the content of the training curriculum and creates an opportunity for the learners to demonstrate real-world application of the content.

In some situations, you may choose to ask the learners to commit to some future action to be implemented upon their return to their real-world work situations. In a workshop focused on sales prospecting skills, the learners might be asked to set 20 prospect meetings from telephone cold calls within the week following the training. This is an effective example because it clearly links the learning to the desired performance in a measurable way. This example would also be an excellent way to integrate frontline management into the training and evaluation feedback loop. In chapter 6, we will explore defining learner outcomes in greater detail.

Step 2: Mindmap the Content

Once you have defined what the learners should be able to do at the end of the learning experience, you are ready to explore what types of content might be included in the training. Begin by mindmapping the information and knowledge you will be delivering. Your mindmap should capture the essence of the content, the details that support the main ideas, and the relationships among them.

Brainstorming, stream of consciousness dumping, and research are the key processes involved in this step. Put everything you can think of on your map, and then start circling the patterns that emerge. Note connections in patterns with colors, symbols, or whatever you find helpful.

This is the part of the process where you synthesize all the information that might be included in the experience. Books, articles, existing training modules, videos, and operating procedures would all fit here. Once you can see all the content, you can easily identify the biggest chunks and how those chunks fit together.

Figure 5-1. Leadership and style mindmap.

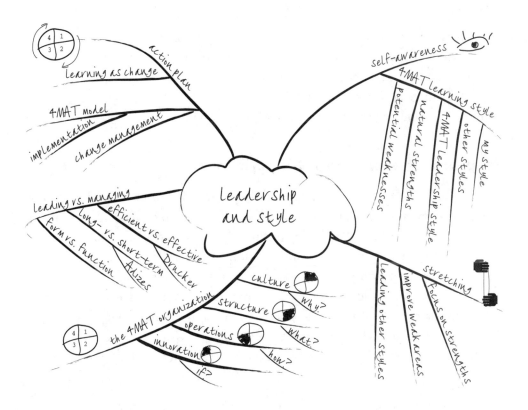

The mindmap example shown in figure 5-1 illustrates content that might be included in a leadership development workshop based on the 4MAT Leadership Behavior Indicator style assessment. This mindmap began with the simple distinctions between different leadership styles that enhance self-awareness. As the brainstorming continued, other content was added that moved the learners from self-awareness to a broader application of style in leadership roles. Stretching exercises, application within organizations, and the distinction between leadership and management functions were also integrated into the content. This led to an exploration of what subject matter experts might be integrated. In this example, the works of Peter Drucker and Ichak Adizes were noted as possible sources of content.

Many trainers are tempted to skip this part of the process and quickly list the content to be included. A well-done mindmap will allow you to see the relationships of the content. The trainer must first see the relationship of the various pieces of content to create an opportunity for the learners to understand the relationship.

The content you define will live in the Inform section of your 4MAT wheel. Begin with how you will convey the content:

- How will you deliver the information to the learners?
- Will you encourage interaction? Will you interact with the learners and ask them to react to what they are learning?
- Will there be assigned readings?
- Will you include subject matter experts?

Step 3: Determine the Concept

You are searching for the common ground that connects all your learners to the material. The common ground is your concept. Concepts are the overarching ideas that hold together the content of a training design. The decision regarding which concept to use depends on the context. Consider the learners, their backgrounds, the culture of the workplace, and what is going on in the world around the workplace. Begin by reviewing the content and looking for a big idea that encompasses all of the content. Next ask yourself, "What is the big idea that comes out of this content, the big idea that will form an umbrella to encompass the content?" Use the answer to this question to create an umbrella, as shown in figure 5-2. Remember, effective concepts

- are core, essence ideas
- form bridges that link the learners' experiences to the content
- have immediate relevance for the learners
- establish relationships between topics.

The umbrella, which is described in more detail in the appendix, is a visual metaphor for describing the method for defining a larger idea that will encompass the specific content being covered. The concept is a connecting idea that holds the con-

Figure 5-2. Content umbrella.

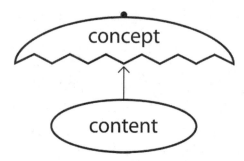

tent together. The most effective concepts build on the experiences of the learners and lead the learners to deeper understandings of the content.

As you are defining the concept, you are searching for a more relational idea, one that your learners can grasp in order to understand the essence of the content with all its details and ramifications. The concept, or big idea, that is the basis for understanding the content can often be discovered by completing the following statement:

(Content) is a study in (Concept).

Following is an example of an umbrella from our designs:

Conflict resolution (content) is a study in win-win (concept).

To emphasize how to turn conflict into an opportunity for growth, we chose "win-win" as our concept. We introduced the training with an analogous exercise in win-win. This concept works well with this content because it begins with a larger idea of mutual gain.

Here are some others we designed:

Creativity (content) is a study in perception (concept).

In this example, we explored and mindmapped references on creativity, both on individual creativity and organizational creativity. We asked, "What is creativity sourced in?" Using the mindmap, we observed that "perception" was a common theme that was reinforced within all the works we explored. This concept expands the idea of creativity from a way of doing things to a way of seeing things.

Coaching (content) is a study in mentoring (concept).

In this example, the concept of mentoring was chosen to reflect the culture of the organization. The concept is effective because it creates an opportunity for the learners to reflect on their own experiences with mentors and explore how they might apply that experience toward coaching others.

Customer service (content) is a study in exceeding expectations (concept).

The concept of exceeding expectations creates many opportunities for the learners to explore their own expectations around service and apply that understanding to servicing their own customers. This concept is effective because it expands the idea of customer service from something the learners do to a larger idea of anticipating and exceeding expectation.

For more help on these first three steps, see the appendix.

Step 4: Complete the Wheel

You will notice that the steps to design a training do not follow the same sequence (Steps 1–8) as those used to deliver a training. The reason is that you need to be clear about your expected results, and then brainstorm and conceptualize your content before you can design your training.

Inform

Fill in the activities you will use to deliver the content of the Learning Cycle. Remember, this is where you deliver the heart of the training. Think lecture, demonstration, and videos. Begin by asking yourself these questions:

- What media can I include to deliver this information?
- Are there subject matter experts whom I can invite into the learning experience to share?
- How might the learners present the information?
- How might I break up the lecture and include individual or group activity?

Practice

Add the activity that you will design to determine how well the learners have learned the skills presented in the Inform step. Think worksheets, role plays, or hands-on application. Begin by asking yourself these questions:

- What can I have the learners do that will allow me to assess their learning of the Inform content?
- What activities will help the learners build comfort with the content before they begin to adapt it for use in their roles?

Connect

Determine how you will help the learners make personal connections to the content. Think personal reflection, simulations, meaningful movie clips, and stories. Begin by asking yourself these questions:

- What is the underlying big idea?
- What concept will these learners most relate to?
- What learner experiences can I draw upon to have the learners relate to the content? How can I elicit these experiences?
- What experience can I create that will allow the learners to explore their understanding of the concept as it relates to their experiences?

Attend

Decide how you will create an opportunity for the learners to process the experience in Connect. Think small groups sharing insights, telling stories, or looking for differences or commonalities. Begin by asking yourself these questions:

- How will the learners process their insights from Connect?
- What task can I assign the learners to elicit reflection and dialogue?
- How will the learners report their experiences to the larger group?

Extend

How will the learners use this learning in their real-life work situations? Here the learners are leading the way, figuring out how they will apply the information. Think role plays, real-life work scenarios, and in-the-field practice sessions. Begin by asking yourself these questions:

- What activity will allow the learners to use the information in ways that are most similar to how it will be applied in their real-life work situations?
- How will the groups or individuals share their work?

Refine

Here the learners refine their work performed in Extend. Think about activities where learners can coach themselves and others or identify ways they might improve the application. Begin by asking yourself these questions:

- How will the learners assess their performances in Extend?
- What key criteria will the learners use to evaluate their learning?

Perform

The learners plan how they will share and celebrate their learning. Ideally, this activity will act as a springboard for future learning. Think sharing of portfolios, presentations, or commitment statements. Begin by asking yourself these questions:

- What activity will inspire the learners to continue this learning application in their roles?
- How will you measure application in the real world? What feedback loop can you design that will support this measurement?

Image

This is a difficult and important step. It attempts to capture not only the core of the content, but also the connection between the subjective insights shared in the first part of the Learning Cycle, Engage, and the objective information shared in the second part of the Learning Cycle, Share. We complete this step last because it often becomes obvious what this step should be after examining the entire wheel for conceptual coherence. Think images, visual organizers, poems, photos, or mindmaps. Begin by asking yourself these questions:

- What images might work to bridge the learner experience in Engage to the content being shared in Inform?
- Are there visual organizers the learners can use to create maps of their insights?
- Will a collection of images for learners to choose from be valuable here?
- Will an activity where the learners create images work here?
- Are there pictures you can provide that will emphasize the concept and prepare the learners for the lecture?

When you complete the entire process, go back through your 4MAT Model and examine it for flow. You want a cohesive, coherent whole. There should be a sense of movement that connects the learners to the content and back to their worlds. When

> "More and more living beings discover what it is to make a shape, an image, to devise a metaphor, to tell a tale—for the sake of finding their own openings."
> —Maxine Greene

the design is done well, the learners should have the sense that the experience is unfolding with each phase of the learning building upon the previous.

Your Learning Workshop: Stretching Your Trainings Using the Eight Steps of the 4MAT Model

Examine one of your own training designs in light of the eight steps described in table 5-1.

Table 5-1. The eight steps in the 4MAT Model.

The Eight Steps	The Learners are...	The Trainer is...	
Connect Create an experience	Establishing a relationship between the content and their personal lives	Constructing/facilitating a learning experience that connects the learners personally	• Stories • Simu • Scenarios tha • Inte
Attend Analyze the experience	Analyzing what happened in Connect, paying attention to similarities and differences of experience	Guiding the reflection, encouraging sharing of personal perceptions and beliefs, connecting the learners	• Quest • Shari • Creat differ
Image Visualize the connection	Seeing the bigger picture of the content that is about to be delivered	Using another medium (not reading or writing) to connect the learners to the underlying concept, transforming the content to be taught into an image or experience	• Choosi being t
Inform Learn the expert knowledge	Receiving information, taking notes, asking questions, discussing	Sharing information and knowledge through lecture, emphasizing the key points through a variety of delivery methods	• Presentations • Lectures • Teams
Practice Practice the expert way	Practicing skills learned in Inform, hands-on use of the information	Facilitating practice activities; providing projects, scenarios, or worksheets	• Role plays • Worksheets • Fiel • Simu • Game show–

Table 5-1. The eight steps in the 4MAT Model (continued).

	The Eight Steps	The Learners are...	The Trainer is...	
6	**Extend** Adapt it to their way	Applying the information learned in a way that is relevant to their real-life or work situations	Setting up situations in which the learners use the skills and knowledge as they would in real-life or work situations	• In-field • Problem- • Role plays • Projects that apply the ski
7	**Refine** Evaluate and refine individual adaptations	Taking ownership of the information by assessing their own progress and performance	Encouraging the learners to evaluate their own application produced in Extend, giving feedback, reviewing key points	• Stories • Simu • Scenarios tha • Inter
8	**Perform** Integrate, implement, and perform	Demonstrating original applications of the learning	Facilitating learning and sharing between learners, giving quality feedback, setting up follow-up and feedback loops	• Dem • Onsite • Sharing commitm • Reports, art share wi • Competency asses

Chapter 6

Learner Outcomes

This chapter will give you a clear picture of how the 4MAT Model Learning Cycle transforms learners. First, the Learning Cycle takes them from their past knowledge into new knowledge. Second, it moves them from their internal perceptions to their actions on their external worlds. Third, the learners move from being receivers of experiences and knowledge to being producers of their own adaptations of what they have experienced and learned.

A power shift happens in the Learning Cycle, as shown in figure 6-1. In the first two parts of the Learning Cycle, Engage and Share, the learners are the receivers. In the last two parts of the Learning Cycle, Practice and Perform, they are the producers, making the learning their own. The power shifts from trainer initiative to learner initiative.

For the learning to be effective, the practice and application in Practice and Perform must be based on skills that will directly affect real-world performance. This is the part of instructional design that is seldom done well. Learning should be immediately applicable to the learners' current work situations.

Learner Outcome Alignment

The best way to make sure that you are aligning the learning with the workplace need is to clearly define the learner outcomes. Learner outcomes are what the learners will be able to understand and do at the end of the experience.

One way to approach defining clear, specific learner outcomes is to conduct a performance gap analysis. You can do this by defining the gap between current knowledge and skill level and desired or required knowledge and skill level to perform the role effectively, as shown in figure 6-2.

Figure 6-1. 4MAT Model wheel.

To define the performance gap, you must know what specifically the learners will do differently and better at the end of the learning experience with your content delivery and skills practice activities. Below are some questions you must answer to do this effectively:

- Are there gaps between the employees' current skill levels and the required skill levels for the jobs?
- What will the learners need to understand to be engaged in improving their skills?
- What information or knowledge do the learners need to understand to improve?
- What do the learners need to be able to do better?
- What will the learners need to understand to assess their progress?

Once you are clear on the performance gap, you can define what specific skills and knowledge the learners will need to gain at the end of the learning session to address this gap. These are the skills that you need to build into your practice activities in Quadrant Three.

Many trainers share that the bulk of the requests they receive for training from frontline managers is more specific on the content, rather than the outcome. It is important that you ask the necessary questions to determine clearly what the desired

Figure 6-2. Performance gap analysis.

outcomes are. Only after you have defined the outcomes, should you move on to exploring what content should be included.

For example, a departmental manager may request a training on accountability. Your first task is to determine what the performance gap is. What did this team need to be able to do better? Simply talking about being more accountable rarely produces the desired result of more accountability. Trainers have to dig deeper and find out why accountability is an issue of concern. Is accountability really the issue, or is it a symptom of a greater issue?

You might ask yourself, the departmental manager, and even the department team members questions such as, "What do people need to do more effectively to be viewed as accountable?" "What prevents this team from operating in an accountable manner?" "Is there something else underneath the apparent issue of accountability that is the real issue?" In this example, you might determine that there is poor communication regarding commitments and deadlines. Poor communication is the source of the perceived lack of accountability. Once you have determined the issue, you can more easily define the performance gap. In this example, the performance gap is defined as, "Employees need to more effectively communicate commitments and progress regarding essential projects and processes."

Based on this gap analysis, you can now begin to clearly define the

> "The major challenge for leaders in the twenty-first century will be how to release the brainpower of their organizations."
>
> —Warren Bennis

learner outcomes. You may find an abundance of skills and knowledge that are associated with being accountable:

- time management skills
- delegation skills
- project planning skills
- communicating skills
- commitment skills.

Based on your performance gap analysis, you have determined that communication is the core issue related to the perception of lack of accountability. The question now becomes, "What do you want the learners to be able to do at the end of this learning experience?" The answer to this question forms the basis of your learner outcomes. An example of effective learner outcomes for this workshop might be as follows:

The learner will be able to

- understand the importance of communicating project status on every assignment
- effectively prioritize projects by asking three key questions on every assignment
- identify red flag areas—potential challenges that might affect follow through
- implement project status update system.

Note: The outcomes are specific, clear, and connected to the real world. The outcomes are focused on skills and knowledge that can be put to use immediately.

Learning as a Strategic Advantage

Well-defined learner outcomes are specific, demonstrable, and clear in scope. These three criteria apply to learner outcomes in a workshop format or learner outcomes for an overall training strategy.

Here is an example of a learner outcome for a company-wide training initiative: In most organizations, leadership clearly defines the desired results (vision) and the strategic initiatives that will lead to these results.

The trainer's role is to translate the initiative into tangible, learner behavior. Here, the 4MAT Model Learning Cycle is most useful. The 4MAT Model leads the trainer through a step-by-step procedure, enabling the key players to answer the questions necessary to carry out the initiative: "Why do we need this initiative?" "What exactly will it entail?" "How complicated and time consuming will the transition be?" "Do we believe the results are achievable and worthwhile?"

The 4MAT Model is useful to examine the health of an organization as well as an instructional model. Organizations need Oneness, Twoness, Threeness, and Fourness to be successful. When you understand the nature of the 4MAT Model quadrants, not only can you see quite easily which quadrants are the strongest in an organization, but you also can readily see which quadrants need improvement.

Quadrant One encompasses the community spirit; Quadrant Two encompasses the planning and strategizing structure; Quadrant Three encompasses the operational side of the organization; Quadrant Four encompasses the evaluation and innovation processes. Review the 4MAT Model organization model shown in figure 6-3. When an organization aspires to be a true learning community, it finds that it is better able to accomplish this by moving through the Learning Cycle and answering the four learning questions:

- The organization builds community by sharing the "Why" behind its proposed strategy.
- The people in the organization know "What" resources to allocate to translate strategy into real-world results by providing tools and training; they are pre-

Figure 6-3. The 4MAT Model organization.

pared to monitor progress through effective feedback loops and ongoing coaching.

- The people understand the answer to the "How."
- The culture of the organization creates and innovates by challenging the status quo with the "If" questions.

When designing a large-scale training initiative, begin by asking yourself the following questions:

- Why is this organization in need of this initiative? What meaning is being felt? Once you are clear about this, you will have your concept. If there is a morale problem, what reason is at the core of it? How will you create the opening Quadrant One activities that will bring people into the sharing of necessary meaning? What will the learners need to understand regarding the "Why" behind this initiative? What will need to be communicated to engage the team members in delivering the desired results?
- What information or knowledge will the employees need access to and what levels of understanding will they need to deliver desired results?
- What skills will the employees need to master to produce the desired results? What feedback loops should be in place to monitor progress?
- What systems will be in place to encourage ongoing improvement? How will progress be celebrated?

In one of our training observations, we matched a training team go through the process of determining learner outcomes using this model. The training department of a healthcare organization was tasked with providing training to all employees on cost reduction.

The group began by determining that the outcome they were seeking was to have every employee empowered to make better decisions regarding behavior that affects day-to-day expenses. As they discussed potential concepts using the umbrella graphic organizer, they settled on the following: Cost reduction is a study in waste.

This insight was an important one. The group members agreed that the notion of waste is a more serious problem at the emotional level. They immediately decided to rename the initiative a waste-reduction campaign instead of a cost-reduction campaign. They chose to rename the initiative because they felt that employees would relate personally to the idea of reducing waste if this linked to employee bonuses. The group had a

"Let us watch well our beginnings and results will manage themselves."

—Alexander Clark

lengthy discussion about different ways that they might engage the employees in waste-reducing actions. One trainer, Sheryl, posed this question to the rest of the team, "It comes down to WIIFM (What's in it for me?). Why should a floor nurse care if we buy too many syringes?"

This question and the ensuing dialogue led the group to determine that employees needed to connect the idea of waste reduction directly to employee benefits. The team then created four learner outcomes:

- Learner outcome 1: Every employee will understand the connection between waste reduction and employee profit sharing and benefits.

What information or knowledge will the employee need to access and understand to deliver desired results? This part of the dialogue focused on what information the employees needed to have to actively engage in waste reduction. Using the cost reports available, four key cost factors were identified that employees had direct control over.

- Learner outcome 2: Employees will understand the four cost factors they affect.

What skills will the employee need to master to produce the desired results? What feedback loops should be in place to monitor progress? The team discussed what new behaviors would be required for employees to shift behavior to affect each cost factor. These desired behaviors formed the basis for the skills-oriented learner outcomes.

- Learner outcome 3: Employees will implement waste-reducing behaviors on a consistent basis.

What systems will be in place to encourage ongoing improvement? How will progress be celebrated? In addition, the training team identified a means for all employees to see their progress. They decided that the company intranet would post a waste-reduction scorecard that focused on the four key factors. Also, the team came up with several ideas to facilitate ongoing momentum of the initiative. One example was to introduce a "Bright Idea" campaign. Employees would be encouraged to submit ideas for waste-reducing measures. Each month, several ideas would be chosen for implementation and the contributing employee would receive a bonus.

- Learner outcome 4: Employees will constantly seek innovative ways to reduce waste within the organization.

The above example illustrates how you can generate the results you want by following the 4MAT Model. By using your knowledge of the 4MAT Model, you can define learner outcomes that will ensure successful transfer that generates desired results.

Begin with the end in mind. Posttraining, what do you want the learners to be able to do better? Define this in writing, and then begin the training design process. Think in terms of measurement. What measurable objectives can you attach to your learning outcomes? We will discuss assessment and measurement in the next chapter.

Your Learning Workshop:
Stretching into Real-World Application

The trainer's task is to design practice that is based on the learner outcomes. There are many ways to create experiences that allow the learners to easily transfer the learning to their current work situations:

- playing roles
- simulating
- reviewing case studies
- planning scenarios
- performing guided practice
- reflecting
- completing worksheets
- analyzing errors
- experimenting
- taking a position
- solving problems
- editing
- resolving contradictions
- collecting data
- finding questions
- publishing results
- making predictions
- presenting
- tinkering with the parts
- creating reports
- relating concepts to the real world
- making diagrams
- performing field work
- interviewing
- demonstrating
- checking evidence
- interpreting information
- creating applications

Chapter 7

Evaluating Your Results

All of the advice on great training design is to no avail if you never find out what happened to your learners. You need to know if they mastered the material and put it to use in their work lives. But most of all you need to know the training results for yourself. Assessment literally means to "sit beside and judge." You need to step out of yourself and observe your work with a critical and candid eye. If you can understand assessment as continuous learning, then you will gratefully accept what you see. All successful assessment is learning itself—concern not only with how they did, but also with how they are doing throughout the training. Do not make the mistake of separating assessment from your actual classroom work. It is integral to and ongoing with the work. Master trainers are assessing all the time, and in the case of the 4MAT Model, all throughout the Learning Cycle.

Training evaluation can be measured through two lenses: effectiveness and efficiency.

Measuring Training Effectiveness

Effectiveness is concerned with how well something works. You can determine how well training works by contrasting the actual learning and performance results gained and the desired performance results.

Training effectiveness can be negatively affected by poorly defined learning objectives and less-than-effective design or delivery. The challenge of poorly designed learning objectives begins in the analysis phase of the development process. Oftentimes, a request is made for a specific training topic by a frontline manager. This requested training topic may or may not be directly linked to the desired performance results. If

> "If judgments of my work are always external, I will be dependent on the judges, not myself."
>
> —Bena Kallick

the learner objectives do not clearly address the root behavioral changes needed to change performance, you can end up with a learning experience that is engaging, but not effective.

Assuming you have properly and clearly defined the learning objectives of the course, the key to evaluating overall effectiveness is found in ongoing assessment of the learning process. Donald Kirkpatrick (2005) has an elegant, well-known, four-level model for measuring training effectiveness from least to most effective, as shown in figure 7-1 laid out in the 4MAT Model Learning Cycle. Here you will find an overview of the four levels:

Level 1—Reaction

Reaction is the perceptions of participants regarding personal value gained from the learning experience.

This level of feedback measures the impression or reaction of the learners to the experience. Every program should minimally include this level of feedback to provide for continuous improvement of the training program.

Examples for collecting this type of feedback are reaction surveys administered onsite, post-program follow-up calls, and email surveys.

Level 2—Learning

Learning is the knowledge, skills, and attitude shifts in the learners.

At this level of assessment, you are moving beyond the learners' perceptions to assess the gain of knowledge and skills. Measurement, at this level, is more difficult.

Figure 7-1. Kirkpatrick's four levels of evaluation in the 4MAT Model.

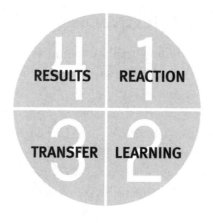

Ideally, you will measure the level of skill or knowledge prior to the learning experience and then measure again after the experience.

Examples for collecting this type of feedback are pre- and post-samples (written tests that include the key concepts of the training).

> "The judgment needs to be internalized. I need to establish the authority of my own voice, to make judgments about my own work."
>
> —Bena Kallick

Level 3—Transfer

Transfer is the learners' changes and adaptations to work life.

Evaluation at this level attempts to determine to what extent the new knowledge or skills are being used in the work environment. The most challenging aspect of measurement at this level is the difficulty in determining when to conduct the assessment.

Examples for collecting this type of feedback are posttraining, onsite observations; post-conference follow-up interviews with immediate supervisors or customers; and reviews of key metrics (re-work, customer complaints, errors, etc.).

Level 4—Results

The *results* level is the linking of learning to increased productivity and higher profits.

This level measures the effect of training on the bottom line. Results-based measurement ties training to the strategic performance of the company.

Examples for collecting this type of feedback are pre- and posttraining measures of

- profitability
- costs
- turnover
- customer satisfaction
- market share
- sales.

Evaluation in the 4MAT Model

The 4MAT Model naturally incorporates all four levels of the Kirkpatrick model. In the 4MAT Model, assessment is happening throughout the learning process, as well as at the completion of the learning process.

We refer to assessment that happens during the Learning Cycle as On-the-Way assessment. By incorporating activities that require learner output throughout the Learning Cycle, the trainer can assess how effective the learning process is during the learning process. This is the only way you can address and adjust the delivery as you move through the Learning Cycle.

For example, in a workshop focused on supporting the learners in making distinctions between leadership and management functions, the trainer may need to assess if the learners understand the key differences between leading and managing. An effective Practice activity might involve asking the learners to create a group Venn diagram that sorts typical leading and managing functions into three categories: leading function, managing function, or both.

The outcome of this exercise allows the trainer to recognize if the learners have enough information to move forward with the learning by beginning to apply it to their real-world work situations. If the outcome indicates that the learners are not yet clear enough on the content to move to application, the trainer can review the content using another method of instruction.

Evaluating training effectiveness in the classroom is an ongoing dialogue between the learners and the trainer, the learners and other learners, and the learners and themselves. As the learning moves into real-world work situations, the dialogue expands to include the frontline manager and the learners' colleagues. The 4MAT Model allows you to create opportunities for the learners to evaluate their learning through their own reflections, their shared dialogue with others, and coaching and feedback provided by the trainer, and the frontline managers.

Take a look at table 7-1, which shows how assessment happens in the 4MAT Model.

Measuring Training Efficiency and E-learning

Efficiency is concerned with the effective use of resources. In the area of training, this involves the process of determining the most efficient method and media for delivering instruction. As the options for delivery continue to broaden with the greater emphasis on e-learning, the question regarding what method and media to use for training delivery becomes more difficult to answer.

The evaluation of e-learning often includes elements that are particular to this delivery medium. Most of the evaluation of e-learning occurs through online data-gathering tools, such as online tests and assessments or devices that record and analyze usage by duration, frequency of log-in, pages accessed, and user profiles.

E-learning, purely from a resource standpoint, can often have major advantages over other delivery methods. While initial development costs can be higher, delivery costs are substantially lower. Time and money saved in e-learning are attractive from an overall efficiency standpoint. To truly determine the effect of e-learning, however, you must look at both effectiveness and efficiency measures.

> "Trainers must create openings that allow participants to dialogue about their own work. They must get people to reflect. They must explore the subtle nuances of their development. This takes a broad range of skills."
>
> —Bena Kallick

Just as we find in trainer-led workshops, the bulk of e-learning evaluation is happening at the Levels 1 and 2 of the Kirkpatrick model. Interestingly enough, many trainers share that participants rate trainer-led programs higher in Level 1. They also tell us that learners generally achieve the same level of results in Level 2, whether online or trainer-led.

The challenge in assessing the overall productivity of e-learning is the general lack of measurement at Levels 3 and 4. In the Practice and Perform parts of the Learning Cycle, ensure that the learners have the ability to transfer and adapt the learning—directly linking to Levels 3 and 4 of evaluation. This is why it is important to include an analysis of both effectiveness and efficiency when evaluating training.

Particularly in e-learning, the evaluation of Levels 3 and 4, learner behavior and results, will happen more frequently in real-world work situations. This means that the alignment between the training function, the learners, and the frontline management is critical.

When you look at organizational learning through the lens of the 4MAT Model, you can easily see how the culture, the structure and systems, the competing priorities and frontline management focus greatly affect how effective learning happens. Take a look at some of the variables that affect training results:

Quadrant One—Why?

- the meaning and importance the learners assign to the learning
- how significantly the learners connect the learning to their lives
- the level of significance the learners' immediate supervisors place on the learning
- the level of support offered posttraining

Table 7-1. Evaluation in the 4MAT Model.

4MAT Model Quadrant	Kirkpatrick Model Level	On-the-Way Learners Demonstrate Learning Effectiveness Through…	On-the-Way Trainer Assesses Effectiveness by Looking for…
1 **Engage**	Reaction—what the learners thought and felt about the training	• Personal reflection • Comparing and contrasting commonalities in experience • Journals, mindmaps, and creating visual aids • Group dialogue, simulations, and study teams	• Observations of learners' interests • Rich dialogue • Acceptance of each other's ideas • Frequency of student-initiated questions • Fluency and flexibility of ideas • Engagement • E-learning: Level of interactivity between learners, frequency of postings, quality of discussion, duration and frequency of log-in, and pages accessed

2 Share

Learning—the resulting increase in knowledge or capability

- Nonverbal representations of connections
- Spatial representations of understanding
- Discussions that provoke deeper understanding
- Fish, Venn, and tree diagrams that illustrate learning
- Constructing models
- Analogies, metaphors, and clusters

- Knowledge clarity
- Questions that indicate understanding and critical thinking
- Comparing and contrasting new knowledge with existing knowledge
- E-learning: Quality of discussion, comparing and contrasting of ideas, integration of other topics, quality of postings

3 Practice

Behavior—extent of behavior and capability improvement and application

- Field work
- Lab work
- Role plays
- Demonstrations
- Worksheets, chapter questions, essays, and articles
- Interviews
- Applying to real-world work situations

- Integration into practical use
- Applying the new learning to real-world problems
- Demonstrating a strong understanding of how to apply the new learning
- Asking questions that support application

4 Perform

Results—the effects on the actual business performance resulting from the trainees' adaptations

- Application to real-world situations
- Adaptation for own use
- Editing, refining, and revising as needed
- Synthesizing new information learned with existing way of doing things

- Extensions of concepts into real-world applications
- Connection to improved effectiveness and efficiency
- Strong grasp of the criteria for evaluating effective learning

Quadrant Two—What?

- competing priorities as defined by the learners and the learners' leaders
- existing systems or conflicting procedures that inhibit new learning
- structure: departments, job descriptions, and reporting relationships that interfere with successful implementation

Quadrant Three—How?

- on-the-job training that conflicts with structured learning
- lack of time for implementation
- lack of ongoing coaching and development

Quadrant Four—If?

- behaviors that are acknowledged or rewarded not aligned with new learning
- promotions, opportunities, or compensation not aligned with new learning
- leadership lack of focus on successful implementation of the new learning

You need to recognize the variables that you have control over, those you have influence over, and those that you have neither control nor influence over. A trainer can design and deliver a powerful and effective learning experience. If the learners must then return to work situations that do not support the learning, either because the frontline managers do not reinforce the learning or because existing systems make it difficult to integrate the learning, the effectiveness measure of the learning will be low.

As you design and deliver training, keep in mind how you address all the factors that can positively, and potentially, negatively affect training effectiveness.

As you develop your 4MAT training designs, include in the Perform step a detailed plan for posttraining follow through. Be sure to balance the type of assessment you use to measure implementation. Solely relying on reaction surveys or learner feedback will give you a limited view of the actual implementation level and effect of the training.

> "There is nothing so useless as doing efficiently that which should not be done at all."
>
> —Peter Drucker

Considerations for an Adequate Implementation Plan

Here are some questions to consider when planning posttraining follow through:
- What are you measuring to evaluate training results?
- Should you gather pretraining data to compare with posttraining results?
- What is the delivery system for follow through?
- Will you be doing all the follow through?
- How much does leadership need to understand about the content to follow through?
- How do you get participants to coach one another?
- Do you need frontline coaches to keep the process going?
- If so, how do you train and interact with those coaches?
- How will the participants be informed of the measurement results?
- Does follow through require one-on-one interaction?
- How can you follow up?
- What media could leverage you? Video? Web? Phone?
- How many review sessions will be required?
- How many trouble-shooting sessions will be required?
- What are the learners to produce?
- How many and what kind of celebrations are planned?

In the next chapter, we will explain how great trainers generate and facilitate energy throughout the entire training course. People's energy levels shift as they move through the Learning Cycle. The quality is subtly different in each quadrant. Your energy as a facilitator must shift to create this flow.

Your Learning Workshop: Stretching Your Assessment Activities

This is a useful assessment tool you can use to review your assessment activities. It is particularly helpful to use at the end of each day in a multi-day training.

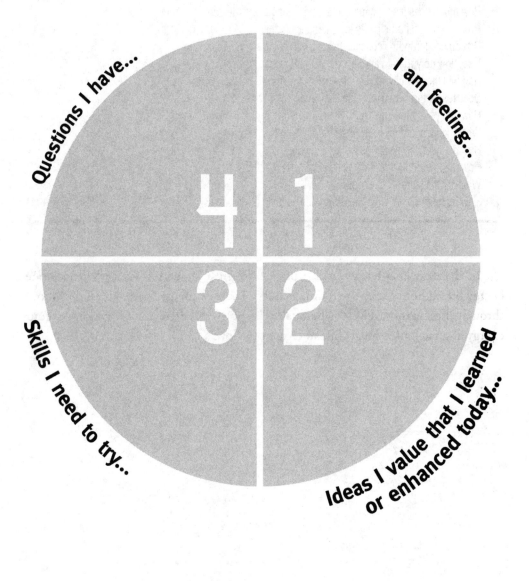

Chapter 8

Improving Delivery Using the 4MAT Model

Designing great training is about defining outcomes and developing learning experiences that will deliver the outcome. Delivering training is about how you execute the design. This final chapter is about the energy you bring to the delivery of training—how to take what you have designed and bring it to life.

Obviously, presentation skills contribute greatly to the ability to deliver engaging learning experiences. Engaging trainers animate the content and activities, effectively bringing the training design to life. As you travel the 4MAT Model Learning Cycle, you are able to sustain energy through the balance of the four parts of the Learning Cycle and the movement between synthesis and analysis. Personal connections lead to reflections and new insights. By combining images with content, you sustain this personal involvement. When you turn the practice activities into personal extensions of the skills, you energize your learners. And the culminating learner performances and implementations guarantee a lasting empowerment. The 4MAT Model is a framework for sustaining high energy in the training process.

When you are delivering training, what are you doing? You are attempting to engage the learners in the learning process. Engaging the learners is the process of focusing energy and holding the attention of the learners. As shown in figure 8-1, we chose the concept of energy for this chapter because the ability to engage the learners is directly linked to your ability to generate, facilitate, and sustain energy in the learning environment.

Think about your own experience of energy in a learning environment, as a learner and as a trainer. Reflect on the questions below:

Figure 8-1. The energy umbrella.

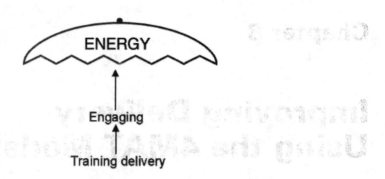

- What is a high-energy learning experience?
- What learning experiences have you had that were high energy?
- Can a learning environment be quiet and reflective and still be high energy?
- Do you have to be a motivational speaker like a Tony Robbins or Stephen Covey to deliver a high-energy learning experience?

By creating experiences that emotionally connect, engage, and challenge the learners, the trainer increases active engagement and, ultimately, retention. A 4MAT Model-based training design naturally does this by creating a balance between reflection and activity. Strong delivery skills are essential to bringing a well-designed training to life. Notice in table 8-1 the different roles the trainer plays in each part of the Learning Cycle and how the learning climate shifts. The learning climate is different in each of the four parts of the Learning Cycle, and the role and delivery style of the trainer is different as well.

Engage—ingage (enter into) to attract and hold by influence or power; to hold the attention of; to induce to participate

To create the learning climate of each part of the Learning Cycle, the trainer must shift the energy of the environment through the delivery approach. Notice in figure 8-2 that when training is done well, the trainer will be more active in the first two parts of the Learning Cycle, Engage and Share. In parts three and four, Practice and Perform, the learners take over and become more active. The techniques you use in the different parts of the Learning Cycle will differ based on the role you are playing and the learning climate you wish to create.

There are many techniques that trainers use to generate and facilitate energy. You generate energy by

Table 8-1. The Learning Cycle climate.

Part of the Learning Cycle	Trainer Role	Learning Climate
Engage	Facilitator	Easy, open, inviting; there is a focus on listening
Share	Deliverer of expert information	Organized, focused, and reflective with an opportunity to ask questions
Practice	Coach	Active with a hands-on, real-world orientation
Perform	Supportive Evaluator	Dynamic, open-ended, challenging, and focused on future implementation and innovation

- creating experiences
- provoking ideas
- asking questions
- challenging thinking
- creating a safe space
- acknowledging
- stretching
- projecting into the future.

You facilitate (move around) energy by

- creating structure
- giving direction
- putting learners into groups
- having learners work alone
- taking breaks
- creating rituals
- changing the physical environment
- redirecting questions.

The key to effective delivery is to choose the right technique at the right time to generate the desired learning climate. We will now explore some techniques that are highly effective for generating and facilitating energy in a learning experience. Because you are seeking to create a different learning climate in each part of the Learning Cycle, we will explore how different delivery techniques work optimally in different parts of the learning process. The techniques we will share can be used to effectively engage the learners at three levels:

Figure 8-2. 4MAT Model wheel.

- socially—engaging through interaction and processing with others
- emotionally—engaging by creating a safe learning environment that encourages exploration and risk taking
- physically—engaging by creating an open, inviting, and comfortable atmosphere for learning.

Ways to Generate and Facilitate Energy in Engage

Energy Quality: reflective, focused, interactive, deep, and personal.

Learners bring prior knowledge with them to the experience. Your role is to structure and facilitate learning experiences that draw out this innate knowledge. Your focus here is attracting the learners, drawing them in, and pulling from their experiences and perceptions. You are leading the process, and the tone you set will be mirrored by the participants. If you want a tone of humor and playfulness, set that tone with the opening of the experience. If the desired

> "Education is a kind of continuing dialogue, and a dialogue assumes different points of view."
> —Robert M. Hutchins

tone is deep, meaningful, and reflective, the questions and activities you choose will determine whether you get this outcome.

Socially

- Ask questions—Good questions provoke thought and expand the dialogue. Think about the questions you ask. In this part of the learning, the questions should be open-ended and draw the learners into participation.
- Allow for reflection—What happens in Quadrant One has the greatest effect on the context of the learning. Your focus is on getting the learners interested by connecting to them personally. Take your time. Be patient. Allow the learners to reflect and share.

Emotionally

- Create a safe space—Learners should feel comfortable asking questions. The idea that there are no wrong answers or stupid questions is often cited in workshops. But often the trainer's subtle language choices undermine the desire to see learners contribute. If you ask for an opinion, then you must acknowledge that every opinion is valid. Even though you might disagree with the opinion, you might choose to respond to a statement that you are not sure about with, "That's interesting, tell me more…." This language tells the learners that the environment is one of exploration with a focus on developing shared understanding.
- Share experiences—You want deep sharing in this part of the Learning Cycle. If the sharing is superficial, then the experience will, ultimately, be superficial. The way you facilitate the process will determine how deep the learning will go. When you are asking someone to share their personal story, it is often effective to begin by sharing your own. This models the outcome you are looking for, and it establishes the depth of the sharing. If you want the sharing to be more personal, your sharing should be personal.

Physically

- Simulate an experience—Engage is a great place to conduct simulations. Games can create powerful shared experiences. These are physical experiences that everyone can use as launch pads to talk about their shared understanding of the concepts you want to explore. Doing a trust fall, where participants lean backward and other team members catch them, would be an excellent physical activity that connects everyone around the idea of trust.
- Change the physical environment—Physical space will affect the quality of the experience. Physical barriers between you and the learners create mental barriers. When you are attempting to connect with people, pay attention to the physical barriers and remove them whenever possible. Some examples of how the physical affects the learners' perception of the learning experience are
  - standing behind podium: "This will be very formal."
  - asking participants to sit facing each other for an exercise, knee to knee: "We will be talking about more personal, intimate stuff now."
  - sitting at the same level as learners: "Oh, we are now in a dialogue, and the trainer seems interested in what we have to say. Now is the time to talk."
  - standing up: "The dialogue is over; now the trainer is going to talk."
  - sitting at round tables: "We will be talking and working together in this class."
  - sitting in lecture-style seating with no table: "All I have to do is listen."

Ways to Generate and Facilitate Energy in Share

Energy Quality: focused, interested, engaged in understanding.

The focus in Share is getting the information across. Here you are focused on creating connections and making sure the learners understand the content you are sharing.

Socially

- Engage the learners in presenting information—Divide the learners into groups, and ask them to read materials and present a section of the lecture. Or send the learners out to interview experts or do research and present their findings. This is often more engaging than listening to one person lecturing, especially when there is a great deal of content to be covered.

- Ask for contribution—As you are presenting new information, the learners are making connections to what they already know. Allow opportunities for the learners to contribute what they know about the content. This could be as simple as asking, "What are your thoughts on this?" to having table groups discuss the big "aha's" or any insights that showed up during the lecture.

Emotionally

- Encourage questions—When a question arises, the learners want it answered. They have a hard time holding all questions to the end of the session. We know that this tactic is often used because trainers don't want to get off track. However, remember that the learners are making connections as the trainer is sharing. The questions are a sign that the learners are not sure how it all fits together. Questions are important; they indicate interest. Even questions that challenge the trainer's position are signs of engagement. Use questions to amp up the overall interest level of the group. Be sure to include the entire audience in the response and weave the question back to the content.
- Validate experience—Encourage and acknowledge learners who bring considerable experience to the learning experience. Look for opportunities to acknowledge learners with a deeper level of the content by asking them to contribute to the sharing of the content.

Physically

- Get comfortable—Let people move around. Make sure the temperature is good. There is nothing more distracting than a learning environment that is too cold or too warm.
- Show the visible relationships—Use images to show how the information connects: diagrams, models, flowcharts, outlines, mindmaps. The more ways you can make the organization of the content concrete, the easier the learning process.

Ways to Generate and Facilitate Energy in Practice

Energy Quality: active, involved, interested.

Socially

- Move people around—When your learners begin to practice the skills learned, trainers should move them around. Rearrange the groups by randomly assigning people by birth month, favorite beverage, or any other method that places the learners in different groups.

- Create options to work solo or in groups—Give learners the option to work alone or work in a group, depending on the task and the desired outcome of the exercise.

Emotionally

- Be clear—Check to make sure that everyone understands by asking, "Have I made myself clear?" or "How did I do on explaining this?" This is very different than asking, "Who doesn't understand?" One puts the burden of understanding on you, and the other puts it on the learners. Feeling like "I'm not getting this," when everybody else is moving on is very uncomfortable.
- Be accessible—When learners are engaged in a task in Practice, walk the room and make yourself available for coaching. Often, when you walk the room, learners will grab you with questions. Rarely will they come to the front of the room to find you. Moving around the room allows you to make sure everyone is on task and moving in the right direction and establishes more intimacy in the learning environment.
- Coach—When you are coaching, your job in this part of the Learning Cycle is to have the learners do the work. Be careful not to take over or give them the right answers. Instead, ask questions. Lead them to discovering how they might approach the task differently. In Practice, you are supporting the learners in building confidence in their understanding. If you continue to provide all the answers, the learners' confidence diminishes.

Physically

- Change venues—This part of the learning could easily be conducted in a new setting. You could send the learners out to do a scavenger hunt or have them move to a lab-type environment.
- Change your position—Be available for questions by constantly moving about the room. Check in on group progress as needed. Pay attention to the process people are using to get to the end product. Observations of the process give you valuable insight to lend to the debriefing of the exercise.

> "The kind of learning that should occur stems from the kinds of questions asked. They should be questions that lead to further questions."
> —The Paideia Group

Ways to Generate and Facilitate Energy in Perform

Energy Quality: engaged, celebratory, inquisitive, open, active.

In Perform, the learners are demonstrating and refining their own learning.

Socially

- Create communities of learning—Create an opportunity or define a medium for learners to continue the learning conversation, after a training. Schedule a posttraining conference call or direct the learners to an online forum to encourage continued interaction.
- Encourage learners to share their learning—Encourage the learners to bring back the learning to their frontline work team. Ask for ideas of how the learners intend to share their insights with their colleagues.

Emotionally

- Allow the learners to assess their work—Create an opportunity for the learners to assess their own performances. After learners share, you might begin by asking, "What insights do you have regarding this process?" and "What might you do differently next time?" Then, move the conversation to the larger audience, "Does anyone else have any insights or thoughts they would like to share?"
- Ask for feedback—Create an opportunity to check in with everyone on the learning process. Feedback slips are a great way to do this. You can also use a mindmap to review the parts of the learning they enjoyed the most and the parts they have suggestions for improving.

Physically

- Change the configuration of the room—The less intimidating the learning environment, the better. You may have everyone pull their chairs to the front of the room or have teams present from their working space. The learners are front and center; the learners are leading the process. In the best of learning, the learners are involved in assessing their own learning and are involved in assessing others' proof of learning. This is where the learners can literally move to the front of the room to share their insights and the products of their learning. Choose to position yourself in a part of the room that allows you to operate as coach rather than leader of the process.
- Present in different venues—Move the performance into the real world. Have the learners present at a staff meeting or some other venue.

- Coach partners—Partner or group people to assess the final product of the learning. Allow each person the opportunity to coach others in the group.

While we prefer to focus on what creates effective delivery, rather than what detracts from it, it is valuable to identify some of the common pitfalls that drain energy in a learning environment. Be aware of these potential pitfalls, and adjust your delivery when you recognize them in the learning environment:

During Quadrant One, Engage, be aware of

- a trainer who talks too much about self
- one person who takes up the talk time
- activities and dialogues that seem to have nothing to do with the content
- conversations that get too personal, too fast
- people who feel forced to share.

During Quadrant Two, Share, be aware of

- a trainer not being clear on where the content is going
- visuals that are neither self-explanatory nor explained
- learners sitting too long
- learners not having the opportunity to interact
- learners not having the opportunity to ask questions
- monotone delivery
- learners feeling stupid for asking questions.

During Quadrant Three, Practice, be aware of

- unclear directions
- activities that seem trivial or have no application to the real world
- waiting too long for other groups to finish
- a trainer who is unavailable to answer questions on the activity
- an exercise that is too hard or missing information.

During Quadrant Four, Perform, be aware of

- learners who feel criticized rather than coached
- a lack of follow through or call for action
- no opportunity to share feedback
- learners who are not all able to share their insights or work
- too much time spent on one part of the process of refining
- a trainer who adds no value in the coaching.

If you are unsure whether any of these potential pitfalls are evident in your training delivery, have a colleague observe your training. Choose someone who will give you strong and honest feedback. Or you may choose to be your own coach by videotaping your delivery. While viewing your videotaped training, notice if any of your techniques are actually draining rather than generating energy. By noticing ineffecctive techniques, you can choose to eliminate them and incorporate others that may work more effectively.

Effective Facilitation of Activities Using Four Questions

Well-designed activities must be well-facilitated for full effect. Giving clear directions and coaching during activities is important to maintaining learner engagement. We find it helpful to prepare for, set up, and facilitate activities by using the four learner questions: "Why," "What," "How," and "If." Notice how answering the four questions will support effective facilitation (see table 8-2).

Transforming from Presenter to Coach

When the learning experience moves from Share to Practice, the trainer shifts roles from information deliverer to coach. The energy of the learning experience shifts considerably and so must your training skills. Your coaching skills will determine the effectiveness of the second half of the learning cycle, Practice and Perform. The 4MAT Model provides an excellent framework for coaching. You should focus on three processes in coaching: observing, asking questions, and encouraging action.

Coaching Is About Observing

Great athletes have coaches that they trust for guidance on the finer points of their performances. The coaches have the ability to see the performances from objective viewpoints and point out subtle strategies for generating greater performance. Think of coaching as the process of observing others and noticing if they are moving toward or away from realizing their potential. Below are ways to become better at observing:

Table 8-2. Effective facilitation of activities using the four questions

If	Why
• Make sure the learners debrief the activity and refine their learning. • Allow time to reflect on the outcome of the activity. • Ask questions that stimulate dialogue. • Connect the learners' insights to the concept of the training design. • Use the insights shared in the debrief of the exercise as a segue to the next step in the 4MAT Model training design.	• Make sure the learners understand why activity. • Connect the activity back to learning experience. Make sure that t connection made between the a and the content you have already c
How	**What**
• Make sure the learners begin the activity. • Define how long they have to complete the activity. • Share how they will be asked to report on the activity to the larger group. • Be present for the learners to ask any questions that may come up. • Walk around the room to make sure that everyone is progressing.	• Make sure the learners are clear on what they will be doing. • Give clear direction on what in the exercise. Before beginning the "Will the learners be doing t they are to be in groups, How will you break the groups up? By month? When they move, will they need to anything with them?" • Clearly communicate wha appropriate, give them an exam you are looking for or the c evaluate the outcome of the exercise.

- Pay close attention to what is happening in the learning experience. Notice how groups are interacting. Who is participating? Dominating? Struggling?
- Take notes as you are watching exercises unfold. Some of the most powerful learning comes from exploring the process the learners used to create the end product of the exercise. Great trainers focus on both process and product in debriefing sessions.
- Ask the learners what they observed about the process.

Coaching Is About Asking Questions

The coach's role is to facilitate the process of identifying behaviors that are not delivering the intended outcome. This means the coach must be skilled at asking questions that help others reflect on their own behavior. When you ask the right questions, the right answers will emerge. Below are some ways to become better at asking effective questions:

- **Design questions in advance**—Focus on what questions you can ask that will allow the learners to discover the answers on their own. This does not mean that you necessarily have the answers. Your role is to be a guide that allows the learners opportunities to think about their own thinking.
- **Demonstrate interest**—As a coaching tool, this works when the questions are based in interest in the learning rather than being interesting as a presenter. Make sure your questions convey authentic interest in uncovering what is to be learned. When trainers ask leading questions that serve only to showcase their knowledge of the subject, the learners disengage.
- **Connect the learning**—Connect it back to the essential question you defined at the beginning of the learning experience. The essential question should be answered at the completion of the Learning Cycle.
- **Focus the learner**—Use questions to keep the entire audience engaged in the debriefing of group presentations. Share with the group the questions that they should be asking themselves as they listen to each group's presentation. For example, "As each group is sharing its presentation, notice which parts have the greatest effect." Encourage the group to observe with keen interest, so that they may participate in the coaching at the completion of each presentation.

Coaching Encourages Action

An effective coach helps to define a strategy for improvement and follows up on progress. Once you acknowledge that there is some room for improvement in the learners' progress with a task or project, be sure the learners are clear on what direction they should take to improve. Below are ways to become better at encouraging the learners:

- Make sure to ask questions that confirm learners are ready to move forward.
- Schedule follow-up times with learners to assess how they are refining the learning in the work environment.

The 4MAT Model easily serves as a framework for coaching learner activities and outcomes:

Perform: Create an opportunity to refine the work. For example, "In your next presentation, what are two ideas you will incorporate to improve your results?	**Engage:** Give the learners opportunities to analyze the experience. For example, "What do you feel really worked well in this project?"
Practice: Offer ideas for improvement. For example, "To make this presentation even more powerful, you might try adding more visuals."	**Share:** Create an opportunity for the learners to analyze what was learned and where they might improve. For example, "What would you do differently?"

Your training style affects the way you coach. To help you further stretch your coaching style, be aware of your natural strengths and be careful not to overuse those strengths. Take a look at the coaching strengths of the four styles.

Strengths of Type One trainers as coaches:

- highly aware of their feelings
- listen well
- speak with empathy
- keep everyone informed and included
- express concerns openly
- have genuine interest in the learners.

Every strength, when overused, can quickly become a weakness. A trainer who overuses the Type One trainer strengths could be described as a Super Nurturer. The Super Nurturer is highly competent at acknowledging others. The Super Nurturer will find all the positive aspects of the learners' work to acknowledge. However, even when pressed for ideas for improvement, the Super Nurturer coach will have a hard time coming up with any. Initially, the Super Nurturer may become the favored coach of the learners because the Super Nurturer always has something positive to say. Unfortunately, over the long term, the learners begin to question the authenticity of the feedback and seek a coach who will help them grow.

Activities a Type One coach might try to stretch:

- Get past the feeling level.
- Ask questions that lead to concrete actions.
- Cultivate the ability to be straightforward.
- Speak to bottom-line concerns.
- Stay with valid data in conflict situations.

Strengths of Type Two trainers as coaches:

- precise and clear
- seldom use exaggeration
- admit when they don't know
- speak only when they are sure
- ask the right questions
- focus on the important data.

A trainer who overuses the Type Two trainer strengths could be described as a Judge. The Judge views the role of coaching as the process of evaluating other's work based on clear standards. When coaching others, the Judge typically focuses on what is less than standard and tends to deliver minimal positive feedback. The Judge may say, "This is not done right..." or "You did not follow directions...." Because the Judge sees coaching as independent from relationships, the Judge has a difficult time understanding why others ask for feedback, but then don't want to hear it.

Activities a Type Two coach might try to stretch:

- Speak to the Big Picture.
- Include possibilities in your communications.
- Share your feelings.
- Ease up on judgments.
- Ask questions that convey an openness to change.
- Consider and honor other people's feelings.

Strengths of Type Three trainers as coaches:

- tell it straight
- get right to the heart and are able to simplify
- communicate more with their actions than their words
- are clear, without ambiguity
- explain things well, step-by-step.

A trainer who overuses the Type Three trainer strengths could be described as the Fixer. The Fixer is a willing coach. The Fixer relishes the opportunity to help others. However, when asked for coaching, the Fixer will often take over the process rather than support the learners in completing the process. Because it is easier for the Fixer to just do it, rather than explain it, the Fixer jumps in and takes over. The learners are left to watch, hoping to learn something in the process. The Fixer is most interested in getting others over the finish line. The Fixer rarely works with learners on the finer points of their work, preferring to say "that's good enough" and move on.

Activities a Type Three coach might try to stretch:

- Pay attention to the learners' feelings.
- Honor the process, as well as the final product.
- Give efficiency and relationships equal balance.
- Suspend certainty.
- Focus on facilitating the learning, rather than demonstrating.

Strengths of Type Four trainers as coaches:

- can see possibilities
- can get others excited
- verbally astute
- communicate their authenticity
- connect disparate things so others can understand
- give genuine praise.

A trainer who overuses the Type Four trainer strengths could be described as a One-Upper. The One-Upper is an enthusiastic coach with lots of ideas for improvement. When the learners come to the One-Upper for feedback, the One-Upper will enthusiastically immerse in the process of generating ideas for improving the learners' work. The One-Upper will often begin by acknowledging the learners for their work, but will often immediately follow the acknowledgement with an idea on how it could have been better. For example, "This is great, but you know what would be even better?" The learners are left with the feeling that none of their work met the standard.

Activities a Type Four coach might try to stretch:

- Listen, really listen, without interrupting.
- Seek to understand before they you to persuade.
- Share with others your thinking process.
- Reflect before you speak.
- Share some of your ideas, rather than all of your ideas.

To help more with stretching your coaching style to appeal to all learners, let's explore what coaching language sounds like in all four parts of the Learning Cycle. Here you will find questions and comments that will stimulate the learners to think about their own learning. The comments are categorized based on the part of the Learning Cycle that they most directly represent. You can use these comments in coaching Practice and Perform in the classroom.

Engage coaching language sounds like the following:

- "Help me understand."
- "Tell me what you are thinking."
- "What are your thoughts on this?"
- "We…"
- "I am concerned."
- "I'm not sure I understand, tell me more about…"
- "What would be helpful…"
- "Tell me what happened, from your viewpoint."
- "Share…"

Share coaching language sounds like the following:

- "What happened?"
- "What we know about this is…"
- "What I observe…"
- "I have noticed…"
- "Have you noticed the reaction you get when…"

- "How do you think this affected…"
- "Why do you think this happened?"
- "What do you believe you are doing that might be contributing to this outcome?"
- "How do you think this was interpreted by…"

Practice coaching language sounds like the following:

- "What would you do differently?"
- "Who do you think is really strong in this area that you could connect with on this?"
- "What action do you need to take first to make a shift in this area?"
- "What do you need from me to support you in this?"

Perform coaching language sounds like the following:

- "What is working?"
- "What else could work better?"
- "What if you…"
- "I suggest you also try…"
- "What ideas do you have that could make this better?"

This framework is also very effective for structuring one-on-one coaching sessions outside of the classroom. Any coaching interaction is a learning experience and, as such, mirrors the 4MAT Model.

Your Learning Workshop:
Stretching Yourself

Enlist a colleague to provide feedback on your presentation style. Videotape your presentations. Review the tapes with a friend. Which part of the Learning Cycle does your presenting style work best in? What parts could be improved? What area do you need to focus on shifting your style?

Become a mentor to other trainers. Nothing gives a bigger stretch than collaborating with a colleague who asks for your help.

Most of all, enjoy the personal growth that the 4MAT Model gives you.

Quick Reference

Strategies for Trainers

Training Strategies for Quadrant One

- Do you introduce your training by setting up situations people can recognize?
- Do you begin with situations that build on what people already know?
- Do you set up situations that draw from people's subjective comments and personal experiences about the training to be presented?
- How often do you construct experiential training situations, that is, simulation or actual experiences where people are involved in something happening, rather than just reading about the topic or listening to information about the topic?
- How often do you set up group problem-solving work to get people into a topic before you deliver training?
- Do you help people to see patterns? How could you do this more often?
- Do you establish the "Why," for example, Why do we need teams at all?
- Why is commitment important in your life outside of the workplace?

Training Strategies for Quadrant Two

- Do you think about the material you use in broad strokes?
- Do you emphasize the underlying rationale of concepts as well as the mechanics? Do you train people not to memorize rules, but to understand the underlying rationale of those rules?
- Do you ask people to explore the relationships among the various sections of your major topics?

- Do you keep returning to the main concept(s) as you move through the training? Do you do so in a way that enables people to see the grace and aesthetics of the concept(s)?
- How often do you ask people to synthesize (overlay and connect various parts) in addition to asking them to analyze material?
- Do you relate your topics to broader social life? For example, "Is this an instance of anything operating today in our culture?"

Training Strategies for Quadrant Three

- Are there elements of absorption, fascination, play, and wonder in this hands-on section of your training?
- Do you set up ways in which people can learn by doing, such as field-based experiences, applications, and information searches that go beyond readings or guided practice?
- Do you require that people test the theories that are presented?
- Do your practice strategies lead to integrated usefulness?
- Do you set up situations that require hunches about possible outcomes, where clues are used as probables rather than the logical adding up of evidence?

Training Strategies for Quadrant Four

- Do you model as a personal value the desire to make a difference in the world?
- Do you ask "If" questions and create "If" situations?
- Do you give many options for people to prove mastery and personal integration of the material presented?
- Do you structure your training design to enable people to redirect their activities relative to their own modified objectives? Do you require that people add their own innovations to the material presented?
- Do you provide situations, relative to your training, that allow people to be involved in open-ended problem solving?
- Is your evaluation designed to include more than factual recall?

Right Mode Training Strategies

These are the strategy characteristics for the right-mode synthesis steps of the 4MAT Model: Step 1—Connect, Step 3—Image, Step 6—Extend, and Step 8—Perform.

Does the activity

- establish personal connections to learning
- encourage people to express their personal viewpoints
- affect people on a feeling level
- use simulations to engage people in learning
- lead people to understand what they may actually have felt
- generate an image or picture in the minds of the learners
- encourage physical or imaginary representations of learning
- give people options for demonstrating their understanding
- promote creative, intuitive approaches to problem solving
- provide setting and background with multiple paths possible
- make substantial use of metaphors
- appeal to the senses?

Right mode activities do not

- require people to know the answer
- attempt to impart knowledge
- rely too heavily on verbal instruction.

At-the-Gate Assessments: Measuring Performance Frozen in Time—Like a Snapshot

In this training design, do you

- test what people know or understand
- measure the quality of what was done
- score or rate mastery
- define the criteria for completion
- ask people to demonstrate what they know?

At-the-Gate assessments usually consist of "-ed" words because the focus is on the past. In these assessments, the trainer will use words like "mastered," "scored," and "described."

On-the-Way Assessments: Dialoguing Ongoing Action— Like a Video

In this training design, do you

- define the elements comprising quality performance

- react to output with an eye to developing it
- provide checkpoints for assessing progress in training
- encourage people to explain in their own words (i.e., how they know what they know)
- assess where people are in the training
- help people overcome obstacles
- help people perfect a process
- ask people to describe what they know?

On-the-Way assessments usually employ "-ing" words, because the focus is on a process. In these assessments, trainers might use words like "progressing," "developing," "advancing," and "mastering."

Appendix

The Critical First Three Steps

The first three steps of the 4MAT Model are critical because the trainer must decide what the concept focus will be, and then create an experiential activity that will encompass that choice to begin. Step two, the Quadrant One, Left Mode step, follows easily if the concept choice is a good one. Group members examine and discuss the experience in some analytic form. Step three, the Quadrant Two, Right Mode step, must reflect the concept experience and analysis in some medium other than verbal, some image form. The images lead the learners right into the knowledge.

Designing Your Own Lesson Plan

Now that we have explored what the learners and the trainer are doing in each of the eight steps, you are ready to begin your own 4MAT training design. To begin, focus on the first three steps of the 4MAT Model. These steps directly connect the learners to the content using a strong concept that the learners understand.

Identifying Strong Concepts

Coming up with a strong concept is the key to designing powerful learning experiences. Previously, we discussed the importance of connecting information to significant concepts. We want to spend some time explaining and practicing the mental process you must go through to identify a concept for your training design.

To begin creating the first three 4MAT steps, we focus on what we call the three Cs: content, concept, and context.

What Are Concepts?

Concepts are the big ideas that are at the core of the content you are sharing. You need only look at advertising, movies, and symbols that inspire you to see the effects of powerful concepts:

Concept and Advertising: Nike and "Just Do It"

Marty Neumeier writes in *The Brand Gap*, "As a weekend athlete, my two nagging doubts are that I might be congenitally lazy, and that I might have little actual ability. I'm not real worried about my shoes. But when the Nike folks say "just do it," they're peering into my soul. I begin to feel that, if they understand me that well, their shoes are probably pretty good."

Concept and Entertainment: *Star Wars* and the Force

"May the force be with you." Utter this famous line and there's no mistaking it. You're referring to the driving force (pardon the pun) behind the *Star Wars* world of exploding planets and intergalactic wars. But what exactly is it? "Ultimately, the message (concept) of *Star Wars* is that the fate of the universe rests on individual choices between good and evil," says *Science and Theology News*.

Concept and Inspiration: *Power vs. Force* by David Hawkins

". . . what inspires us in the physical world are things that symbolize concepts with powerful meanings for us. Such symbols realign our motives. . . . A symbol can marshal great power because of the principle that already resides within our consciousness."

The content is the lecture, or key information you are trying to impart. The concept is the overall meaning of the content, the core of it, the essence of what you are trying to convey. The context is the way the information is framed—the intention, the feeling, the experience, the climate, and the tone.

To create a good concept, you must be clear on the content you are teaching. We suggest that you get all the content down on a piece of paper in "big chunks." Mindmapping is an excellent way to visualize how the different topics you cover connect to one another. Once you've laid out all the content, ask yourself, "What is all this really about? What is the common thread that holds it all together? What is the essence of it?"

A helpful technique we use is to fill in the following statement:

<u>(Content)</u> is a study in <u>(concept)</u>.

For instance, you might be developing a workshop on documentation procedures. The exercise might look like the following:

<u>Documentation</u> (content) is a study in <u>clarity</u> (concept).

Talk-Story on Getting the Concept with Jeanine

Talk-story is a Hawaiian expression for sharing a personal story to illustrate a concept or idea.

I have heard and used the phrase, "Oh, she just doesn't get the concept" many times in my life. I have applied it to all kinds of things from the concept of friendship to the concept of punctuality. It wasn't until my daughter, Madison, shared her own frustration in "not getting the concept" that I really understood what concept is really about.

Madison was in the process of learning her multiplication tables and long and short division. She studied her times tables, and we practiced with flashcards a couple of nights a week. She sailed through all her tests on multiplication tables.

Then, she learned how to do division. Every night, the teacher would send home worksheets with problems like 9 divided by 3 =___? Madison did her practice homework and made As on her weekly quizzes.

Then, one night, she came home, sat at the kitchen counter, and burst into tears. She said she had made a "big, fat zero" on her math test on division. When I looked at the test, I saw that the teacher had said, "Answer the following problems, and show your work." The problems were worded like, "Matt has nine apples. He wants to share them equally among him and his two friends. Show how Matt can figure out how to equally share the apples." Madison had written random numbers on some of the problems and left the others blank. When I asked her what happened, she said, "I have no idea how to figure this out. I don't know how to do this."

Suddenly, I realized she had memorized the multiplication tables and memorized the process of doing division on paper, but she had no idea about what was actually happening in the process. She did not relate to the underlying concept of multiplication and division. She didn't get the concept.

I took nine pennies from my purse. I asked, "If you had to share these nine pennies equally with two of your friends, how would you do it?" She quickly moved the pennies into three piles of three. I looked at her and said, "This is division. You just divided nine pennies by three." She looked at me with amazement and said, "You mean division is splitting things up? Oh my gosh, all this time I had no idea what Miss Kathy was talking about."

Spending time on the front end of the learning experience exploring the underlying concept makes the learning more engaging and more effective.

Another example might be a workshop on leadership development. Figure A-1 shows how a 4MAT trainer uses the 4MAT Model to conceptualize leadership by connecting the learners to their own experiences. The content to be taught is placed in the center of an oval.

Leadership is a study in alignment. Now draw an umbrella over the content oval, symbolizing the bigger meaning—the overarching idea. Write in the word, "alignment," as shown in figure A-2, which forms a more concrete connection to leadership.

Figure A-1. Defining the content.

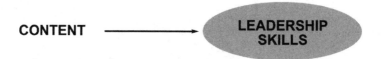

This is a way of visualizing how the concept of your training becomes the overarching idea that holds together the content in a meaningful way.

The concept you choose becomes the glue that holds your training design together. Obviously, different concepts will affect the learners' experiences differently. We facilitated a leadership retreat for a regional banking group. The group was focused on developing a curriculum for a leadership training program for all of their locations. The process of defining the learner outcomes for the program was proving difficult. The two senior leaders of the group had different ideas of what a leader should be able to do effectively. To shift gears, we used the concept exercise with the entire group: Leadership is a study in _____.

Not surprisingly, the two senior leaders had different ideas of the essence of leadership. One leader responded that leadership is a study in control. The second leader responded with leadership is a study in persuasion, as shown in figure A-3.

Obviously, working from different concepts will lead you to different ideas on what content and activities should be included in the training design. Different concepts will also affect the context—the tone or feeling of the learning experience. In this example, the dialogue created around this exercise led the group to choose the concept, synergy.

Figure A-2. Creating a concrete relationship.

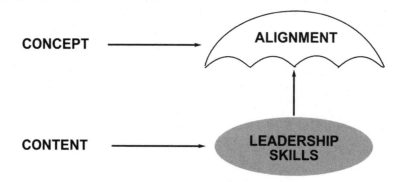

Figure A-3. Using the umbrella to determine learner outcomes.

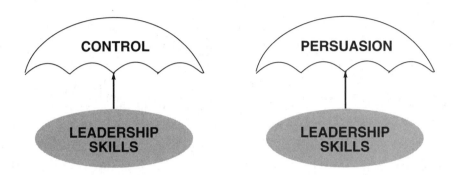

The concepts you choose will become the decision filters for activities you create in your 4MAT training design. The concept holds together all the content you teach, creating a structure for design and delivery.

The First Three 4MAT Model Steps

The conceptual coherence of your training is created in the first three steps of your 4MAT Model. These are the crucial steps for people in training. Every high-impact learning experience includes these major elements. When done well, the learners are immediately engaged in the learning experience and the trainer's job becomes much easier.

The first three steps are

1. Connect
2. Attend
3. Image.

Step 1: Connect—Create an Experience

Engage the learners, starting with where they are. Create an experience that has emotional appeal and is highly motivating. Help people see how valuable learning will be. Create an experience that will create authentic dialogue, no explaining of the con-

Conceptual coherence of your training design and delivery refers to how well the experience flows. Using a strong concept to hold together the content and activities addresses several key brain-based learning issues:

- Learners learn by connecting one thing with another.
- Learners need to see how it all fits together.
- The big ideas (concepts) and the details (topics) must be linked.

tent allowed. This opening step needs to be experiential. No telling; something must happen to them personally.

Movie clips are excellent Connect activities because they tell stories and encourage people to relate their own experiences. In a leadership workshop using the concept of focus, you might begin with a clip from the movie *City Slickers* featuring Billy Crystal. Billy Crystal's character, Mitch, is a forty-something radio ad salesperson questioning the meaning of life. In a particular scene in the movie, Jack Palance's character, a trail boss for a cattle ranch, explains to Mitch that the secret to life is one thing. Mitch replies by asking, "What's the one thing?" Palance's character replies, "That's what you have to figure out." After sharing the video clip, you might ask the learners to share what they believe the one thing is in their organizations.

Step 2: Attend—Analyze the Experience

Now have people discuss and analyze the initial activity. They need to share their perceptions, their reactions, and any relevance the experience had for them. Commonalities can be listed and characteristics discussed.

Building off the example of the *City Slickers* movie clip, ask the learners to reflect in groups on what they believe is the one thing that is most important in their organizations. Have them write the one thing on an index card.

Step 3: Image—Visualize the Concept

The learners visualize the concept formed from the Connect activity in Step 1: an image that will take them directly into the content to be explained in the lecture that follows. An example might be a diagram of a relationship or an illustration of conflicting opposites present in a particular dilemma. This step precedes the lecture, the information piece, and brings the learners from their past directly into the content. The image process enhances their content understanding at a conceptual level, which is exactly what you want.

Using the previous example, ask the learners to place all the index cards on a table with the comments facing up. Have everyone in the group walk around the table and view the differences or similarities in the perception of what the one thing is perceived to be in an organization.

You know the Image step is strong when

- learners are engaged in really thinking about what the concept means
- the product of the activity is different for every learner or small group
- the sharing of the product adds richness to the dialogue and creates a fuller understanding of the concept for everyone

Figure A-4. Concept possibilities for policies and procedures content.

- learners can connect what they do in Image to the information you are about the share in Step 4, Inform.

The Image step is one of the most critical parts of the Learning Cycle. It is also one of the more difficult parts to master as a trainer. If the learners are not given time to create a mental space for new information, they will waste valuable time trying to figure out how this fits into what they already know. Images help the learners to see the bigger concept. So much of training involves building anticipation or romancing people into wanting to discover the information. The question you must ask is, "How can I create an imaging experience that will develop a big picture understanding of the concept?"

Examples of the Steps

If you were creating a training module for explaining corporate policy and procedures (the content) for newly hired employees, what might the overriding concept be? What connection to meaning could you make for a recitation of the rules and the exceptions to the rules that comprise the policies and procedures material? What is the "Why" you could present that could create meaning for the participants?

Figure A-4 shows some concept possibilities for policies and procedures content:

Which one appeals most to you? Is there a better one not listed here? Whichever concept and bridge you choose, it will become the linchpin of your 4MAT Model; it will become the central, cohesive element. It is the glue that holds it all together. Clearly, equally talented trainers could disagree on which of these might be best to capture the essence of a good policies and procedures module.

Which would be the best in your mind for a strong 4MAT Model training design? You can narrow the options by noticing how the conceptualization you choose creates a tone. This tone speaks to the contextual feel of the experience.

To conceptualize policies and procedures with the concept of Your Impact on Us implies a welcoming, a relationship that affects everyone, not just the new person. It sets a tone of people-connectedness and community.

The concept choice of Systems implies a more formal arrangement, an efficiency, with more emphasis on order.

The concept choice of The Way We Do Things Around Here has a down-to-earth tone and implies a system, but there is an emphasis on a more informal culture—one you do not mess with.

This, of course, is the context issue: who your learners are and the climate you choose. You want to choose a concept that aligns with both the content you are teaching and the context you want to have people embrace.

Let's look at another example of the two umbrellas. Imagine you are asked to teach a professional dress code workshop for new employee orientation. The objective of the workshop is to have employees understand the organization's dress code. The content is appropriate clothing choices.

If you explore the conceptual umbrella for the dress code content, you might decide that dress code is about making the right impression. Could that be the concept? What is impression about? Is there something else that is bigger or more powerful than impression? Impression is about making a judgment based on how a person looks. Judgment could be a powerful concept choice for a training in dress code.

Let's walk through the process of designing a workshop on dress code (the content), as shown in figure A-5, using the concept of judgment. Remember, we first went to impression in our brainstorming and then landed on judgment. Imagine the process as peeling the onion until you get to a concept that you feel is really strong.

Now, imagine you are presenting this workshop. How do you connect the content of dress code to the concept of judgment? Ask yourself, "How do I connect the learners personally to what it means to be judged or to judge others?" There are several ways you could approach this. You might ask people to share an experience of when they felt judged based on their appearances. Or you could create an experience where they would have to judge others. Let's look at how the first two steps of this training design might look:

Step 1: Connect—Create an Experience

You could show images of people. The clothing of the people could vary widely in the images—professional clothing, revealing clothing, more make-up, less make-up. In small groups, ask the learners to describe who these people are, what they are like, and what they do for a living.

Figure A-5. Concept possibilities for dress code content.

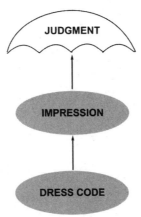

Note: The trainer is simulating an experience of how the learners quickly move to judging others based on appearance.

STEP 2: ATTEND—ANALYZE THE EXPERIENCE

The debrief of the exercise, the sharing of perceptions from Step 1 would create an opportunity for participants to explore the judgments they made based solely on appearance. Ask the learners to share what they noticed about their perceptions. Ask them to note commonalities in their reactions. Facilitate a dialogue on judgments they make as customers.

Note: The learners are talking about the experience. They are noticing the judgments they made and exploring why they made them. The learners are becoming more personally connected to the idea that everyone judges based on appearance.

STEP 3: IMAGE—VISUALIZE THE CONCEPT

After the learners share their experiences around judgment and record common characteristics, you are ready for Step 3. What can you do to help the learners visualize the concept of judgment? In this 4MAT Model step of imagining the concept, you might ask each small group to assume three roles. You could ask, "If we want to appear as an intellectual, a down-home type, or a sensual type, what kinds of looks might be effective?" From a collection of images, have the groups choose images that convey each type of impression. While this activity is great

> When you create an effective Image experience, the learners arrive at the Inform part of the Learning Cycle ready to learn.

fun, it also probes deeper into the human experience of wanting to make a good impression.

Note: This exercise moves people closer to the content. This activity also bridges the gap between the personal experience of judging and employee dress codes. Now, the learners are ready to talk about the impression their organization wants to convey to customers and how dress code affects that impression.

Your Learning Workshop: Stretching Exercises

Effective design of the first three steps of the 4MAT Model takes practice. Start paying attention to what experiences you create that truly engage the learners in a meaningful dialogue. Notice how often you begin with some experience that does not involve telling the learners.

Next time you watch a movie, see if you can sum up the concept in a word or two. Try asking a few friends to summarize a movie in a word. Notice how different concepts can be equally effective.

References

Berlin, I. *The Hedgehog and the Fox*. Chicago: Elephant Paperbacks, 1993.

Collins, J. *Good To Great: Why Some Companies Make the Leap ... and Others Don't*. New York: HarperCollins Publishers, 2001.

Costa, P. T., Jr., and R. R. McCrae. *NEO PI-R Professional Manual*. Odessa, FL: Psychological Assessment Resources, 1992.

Dewey, J. "How We Think: A Restatement of the Relation of Reflective Thinking to the Educative Process." *John Dewey: The Later Works, 1925–1953*, J. A. Boydston, editor. Carbondale, IL: Southern University Press, 1986.

———. *Experience and Nature*. New York: Dover Publications, 1958.

Diamond, M. C. *Magic Trees of the Mind*. New York: Dutton Books, 1998.

Eisner, E. *The Enlightened Eye: Qualitative Inquiry and the Enhancement of Educational Practice*. New York: Macmillan, 1991.

Greene, M. *Releasing the Imagination: Essays on Education, the Arts and Social Change*. Hoboken, NJ: Jossey-Bass, 1995.

Harvard Conference. *Learning and the Brain, Motivating the Mind, Using Brain Research to Enhance Student Performance*. Boston: Public Information Resources, 2005.

Hawkins, D. *Power vs. Force: The Hidden Determinants of Human Behavior*. Carlsbad, CA: Hay House, 2002.

Jung, Carl. *Psychological Types*. Princeton, NJ: Princeton University Press, 1976.

Kirkpatrick, D. L. *Evaluating Training Programs: The Four Levels* (3rd edition). San Francisco: Berrett-Koehler Publishers, 2005.

Kolb, D. A. *Experiential Learning: Experience as a Source of Learning and Development*. Englewood Cliffs, NJ: Prentice-Hall, 1983.

Lawrence, G. D. *People Types and Tiger Stripes*. Gainesville, FL: Center for Psychological Types, 1993.

Lewin, K. *A Dynamic Theory of Personality*. New York: McGraw-Hill, 1935.

Luria, A. *Higher Cortical Functions in Man*. New York: Basic Books, 1962.

McCarthy, B. *About Teaching*. Wauconda, IL. About Learning Inc., 2000.

———. *About Learning*. Wauconda, IL. About Learning Inc., 1996.

Neumeier, M. *The Brand Gap*. Berkeley, CA: New Riders, 2003.

Piaget, J. *Psychology and Epistemology: Towards a Theory of Knowledge*. New York: Viking Press, 1972.

Polanyi, M. *The Tacit Dimension*. Gloucester, MA: Peter Smith, 1983.

Restak, R. *Mozart's Brain and the Fighter Pilot: Unleashing Your Brain's Potential*. New York: Three Rivers Press, 2001.

Senge, P. M. *A Fifth Discipline Resource: Schools that Learn*. New York: Doubleday, 2000.

Siegel, D. *The Developing Mind: Toward A Neurobiology of Interpersonal Experience*. New York: The Guilford Press, 1999.

Surowiecki, J. *The Wisdom of Crowds: Why the Many are Smarter than the Few and How Collective Wisdom Shapes Business, Economies, Societies, and Nations*. New York: Doubleday, 2003.

Vygotsky, L. S. *Mind in Society*. Cambridge, MA: Harvard University Press, 1978.

Zull, J. E. *The Art of Changing the Brain: Enriching the Practice of Teaching by Exploring the Biology of Learning*. Sterling, VA: Stylus, 2002.

Index

(Page numbers in italic refer to boxed text, illustrations, or tables.)

in learning process, 13–14
sharing learning style and, 15
trainer's assessment of questioning
style, 22
why? questions, 9–10
for effective facilitation, 98
engaged learning and, 15

goals, 14
in learning process, 13–14, 19–20
trainer's assessment of questioning
style, 22

Z
Zull, James, *24, 31, 47*

About the Authors

Bernice McCarthy

Bernice McCarthy received her doctorate from Northwestern University in education and is one of the founders of the learning styles movement. She is the creator of the 4MAT Model, an innovative, research-based teaching model that is being used by organizations worldwide to improve learning effectiveness. Her teacher training has been introduced into thousands of school systems, both public and private. She has presented numerous workshops and keynote sessions on effective learning at renowned organizations, such as Northwestern University, Cornell University, Lehigh University, and the University of Houston, as well as consulted with the U.S. Navy, the Smithsonian, IKEA Furniture, the National Institute of Corrections, and the Peace Corps.

Jeanine O'Neill-Blackwell

Jeanine O'Neill-Blackwell understands the way training happens in the real world. She has nearly 20 years of experience as a sales trainer, corporate trainer, senior-level human resources leader, and president of a corporate university. As a partner in a school management company, she has designed and implemented large-scale, train-the-trainer initiatives. As president and CEO of 4MAT 4Business, she delivers tools, consulting, and training for leaders and trainers focused on improving learning design and implementation in organizations.